Jacobus Community Park

Jacobus, PA

Doug Arnold

HOMEMADE PUBLISHING

Homemade Publishing

Jacobus Community Park - Jacobus, PA/ Doug Arnold. -- 1st ed.

Hardcover ISBN 978-1-7322532-0-9
Softcover ISBN 978-1-7322532-1-6
E-book ISBN 978-1-7322532-2-3

To the Boys of Summer who became our Fathers

CONTENTS

Introduction 1
Beginnings 7
Back in Business 19
High Jinks in Town and other Stories 29
Strawberry Fields 35
The Jacobus Athletic Association 39
Play Ball! 47
Building the Legacy 65
The Money Game 99
High Jinks on the Road 109
Kaboom! 117
Swinging for the Fences 123
The Big Day 139
Celebrating the Good Old Days 143
It Ain't Over Yet 147
Sources 153
Appendix A: Purchase of the Property 157
Appendix B: Jacobus Athletic Association Minutes 171
Appendix C: Teams and Leagues 241
Appendix D: Trophy Case 253
Appendix E: The Roster (Early 1900's to early 1970's) 271
Appendix F: Local Baseball Dynasties and the Arnold Family 315

Introduction

Don't look back. Something might be gaining on you.

— Satchel Paige

Spring 2018

It's a good sign that you're losing interest in baseball when you can't recognize the names of any of the players elected to the Baseball Hall of Fame for the current year – but it wasn't always that way…

There was a time, fifty-five or so years ago, when my friends and I could name all of the players on the Baltimore Orioles baseball team without breaking a sweat. I still have a program from the 1966 World Series. I was not at the World Series that year, but this was a souvenir made available to members of the "Junior Orioles Club". We wore Orioles baseball hats and my one brother even had a kid's Orioles batting helmet. I can probably still name a player from each position from the Orioles teams from around that time. Now I can't even guess at the positions that the new Hall of Fame inductees played. My brother used to inhale every baseball book he could get his hands on and is still a master of baseball history, players, and stats from those days. Over the years things have changed and I can't pinpoint exactly when I started to lose track. Interests change and life starts to get in the way.

There was a book released in 1987 at the time of the Jacobus, PA sesquecentenial (150th year) celebration called ***Jacobus, Pennsylvania (New Paradise) 1837 – 1987***, published by Mehl Associates. There's a chapter in that book that describes baseball in the early 20th century in Jacobus. It mentions that; "Since the turn of the century, baseball has been an important part of this town's recreation, if not the chief organized sport. As the first Major league records begin in 1901, baseball was not slow catching on in the village of Paradise (Jacobus), as shown by the accompanying picture of the team that played here in 1908, managed by Ed Wolf.". As described in that chapter, those early teams played games at some of the farm properties in Jacobus.

1908 Jacobus Baseball Team - This photo was supplied by George Keeney Jr. and appeared on page 31 in the "Jacobus, Pennsylvania (New Paradise) 1837-1987" sesquicentennial book.

In addition, this photo appeared in the York Daily Record Newspaper with the following caption – "Jacobus' first baseball team as they appeared on Sept. 12, 1908, in Yoe, included, front from left (no first name available) Arnold and Bill Myers; second row, Harvey Myers, Saul Shearer, Ed Wolf, Ed Darr and Addision Shearer; and third row, Bert Dellinger, (no name available), Sal Rohrbaugh, N.J. Leader and Lester Loucks."

Now for some reason I find myself in the position of continuing and expanding on that history. The days are flying by and I see that it's time to write some things down. Contrary to what Satchel Paige recommends, that's the purpose of this book. It will weave some personal threads of my own, and more importantly, threads from the stories of hometown heroes.

The time period covered here will be mostly from the late 1930's to the mid 1970's. This is for two reasons. First, after the early 1970's, I missed out on many of the things that went on back home in Jacobus and at the park, since I've lived out of the area much of the time since then. The second reason is that forty years is a long enough period of time to research and write about in one book. I will leave it to someone else to continue this history in the future.

I'm standing at home plate in a baseball park in my home town of Jacobus, PA. There's a nice grass field, dugouts, bleachers, a backstop, a scoreboard, and all of the other things that make up a baseball park. Across the way are pavilions, a tennis court, and children's playground equipment. Every summer this place is filled with sound and activity of all kinds. Down the road someone else standing here may wonder where all of this came from. This book is the story about where it came from.

Jacobus Community Park, catcher's eye view – Fall 2017

Jacobus Community Park, view from the home team dugout – Fall 2017

Jacobus Community Park, the recreation area – Fall 2017

Beginnings

Baseball gives every American boy a chance to excel, not just to be as good as someone else but to be better than someone else. That is the nature of man and the name of the game.
— Ted Williams

1930s

It is an exciting time for baseball during the first few decades of the 20th century. Interest in the game is taking off in America with greats such as Babe Ruth in the national spotlight. Everything about the game is increasing in popularity, and then things take a wrong turn. In the early 1930s, the Great Depression causes a lot of the fans to have to turn their attention instead to just keeping their lives and livelihoods going.

Thankfully by the end of the 1930's, things are finally starting to turn around again. A handful of heroes are taking baseball to a new level of popularity, and the country is more than happy to start turning its attention away from the Depression. In New York there is a veteran first baseman named Lou Gehrig and a rookie centerfielder named Joe DiMaggio, who are both making their marks playing for the Yankees. In Boston, another player, who is to become one of the greatest players of all time, Ted Williams, is just beginning his career with the Red Sox. Major League baseball legends are becoming national heroes. The heroes are in place, and just about every kid in the country wants to learn the game and to take their best shot at being the next big star. Baseball fever is in the air, and the kids and young men in Jacobus, PA. are not immune…

At the end of the 1930's, the population of Jacobus, PA. is around 500. Route 111 is the Main Street in town and it runs the length of town north to south. Starting at the south end of town and heading north, there is mostly farmland and a schoolhouse for kids grades 1 through 8. To the west of Route 111 run two main roads. Seven Valleys Road runs west, a few blocks north from the south end of town, and continues on to the town of Seven Valleys. It has mostly farmland on both the north and south sides, with a scattering of houses along the way, including the Anstine house and the Hengst farmhouse. A little farther north along Route 111, at about the middle of town, Water Street also runs west out of town. Along Water Street, not too far out of town, is Lake Williams, which provides a water supply for the surrounding area. Between Seven Valleys Road and Water Street, on the west side of Route 111, is the Smith Village store complex, including cabins for rent, a restaurant, and an Atlantic gas station. On the southwest corner of Water Street and Route 111 is Innerst Auto Company and on the northwest corner stands Curvin Kohr's Grocery store. Heading to the north end of town, then across the street, to the east side of Route 111, there is Myer's Blacksmith shop. Starting at the north end of town at the Blacksmith shop and now traveling south on Route 111, there are two main roads running east. A few blocks south from the north end of town, Church Street runs east toward the Lutheran Church. One house north from the northeast corner of Church Street and Route 111 is Goodling's variety store. Across Route 111 from Goodling's store is the Evangelical Church. One house south from the southeast corner of Church Street and Route 111 is Mickley and Olp's Flower shop. Continuing south along Main Street toward the south end of town again, and directly across Route 111 from Seven Valleys Road, is York Road. York Road runs east out of town and then runs parallel to Route 111. York Road meets up with Church Street at the Lutheran Church. Between Church Street and York Road on the east side of Route 111 is the first Jacobus Fire Station, Leader's Furniture Store, and an Esso gas station. That's the quick tour up and down Main Street Jacobus as things are in the late 1930's.

Jacobus Community Park - Jacobus, PA

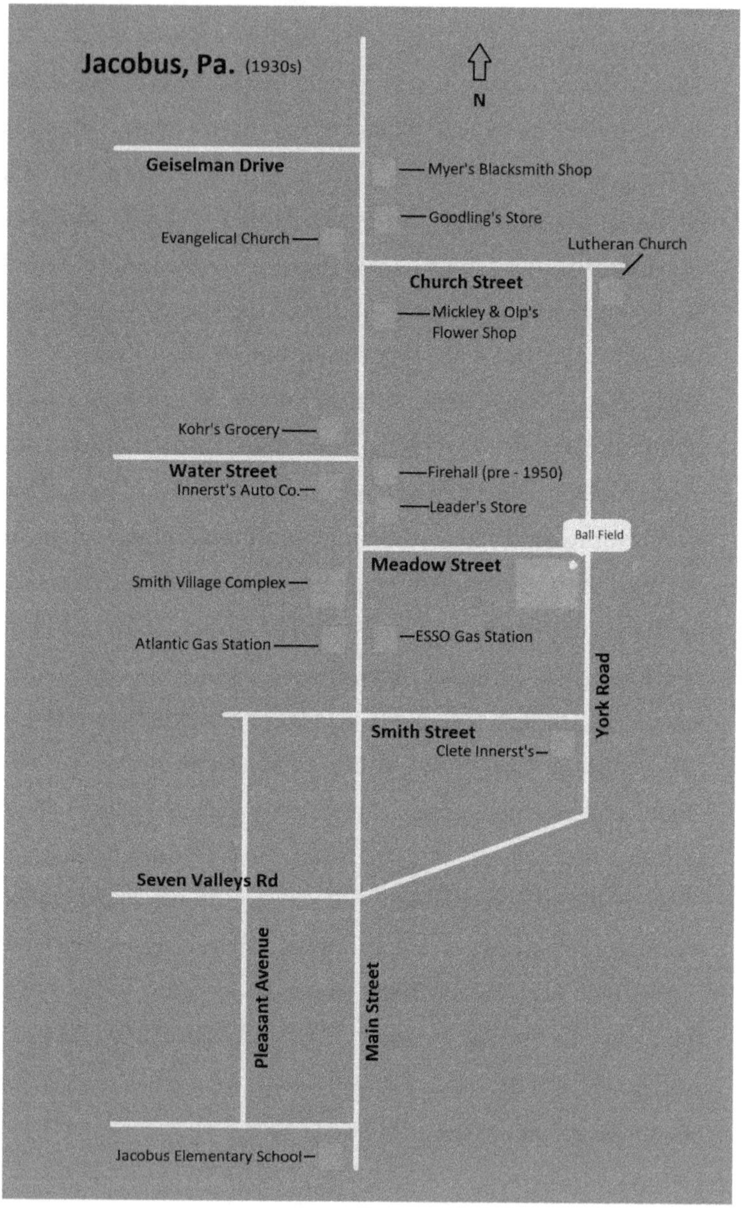

On baseball game day, crowds begin to gather early at the baseball field at the southwest corner of York Road and Meadow Street in Jacobus. Meadow Street, which runs along right field, is a narrow street connecting York Road and Main Street in town. It runs across a small creek to Sol Shearer's residence along Main Street. Home plate is located right in the southwest corner of that intersection. Left field runs south along York Road into the cornfield at the property of Clete Innerst. Clete Innerst's business does construction work, road work, and snow removal around town. Center field runs up behind the Esso gas station property.

It helps to get there early to reserve your seat and to see a little of the pre-game warm-ups. Even though there are a few seats in the bleachers behind home plate, most of the seating is "bring your own" chair or blanket seating.

Even for grade school kids, it is exciting to attend the games there. You get a nickel for running after foul balls. Most of the kids know that the Kornbau property, across York Road from the left field line, is usually "off limits" for a kid to try and get a foul ball that lands there. If a foul ball goes onto the Kornbau property, most of the time, one of the Kornbau family is out in the yard to claim the ball. No matter, there is always competition and wrestling for a foul ball among the kids. At times, a foul ball will break a car window, since cars park along York Road, near the ball diamond. As a kid, getting one of those foul balls back, after it breaks a car window, is even tougher than getting one that lands on the Kornbau property.

Thinking about that time, my uncle Lee Arnold recalls, "We had uncles that played baseball around that time and we all became interested in playing. They played for different teams in the county. Back in those days baseball was your life." It seems then that if you had any athletic ability you played ball, and if you didn't, you supported and helped out the team in whatever way you could. And so, the generation that would play in the 40's and 50's was already learning to love the game, while they chased down foul balls.

Around this same time, there were two players from the area who were fortunate and talented enough to begin the climb into the professional baseball leagues. Bill "Heine" Heltzel played with the Boston Brave's organization 1935 – 1947. He played at the major league level in 1943 – 1944. Sterling Arnold played in the St. Louis Cardinals minor league system 1938 – 1940. My uncle Bob mentioned, "Sterling was wounded in the war (WW II) and had a number of bones broken in his leg. He lost his ability to play professionally because of the injury". According to my uncle Ted, "Even after the injury to his leg, 'Sterl' was still good enough to play in the local leagues. He pitched for Red Lion for a while after he got out of the service. They would put in a pinch runner for him if he got on base, because of his leg injury."

The Jacobus "Reserve" team was league champions in 1938. Unfortunately, at the end of the 1930s, World War II took people's attention away from baseball once again, just as the

Great Depression had done a few years earlier. During the war, a lot of towns stopped having teams, Jacobus included. A lot of the players went into the service. During the war years, baseball was discontinued and the property at York Road and Meadow Street was gradually divided into lots for homes. At the same time, there was also an expansion of Clete Innerst's business and the Smith Village store complex. Soon there was no longer any room for a baseball field at the York Road and Meadow Street location.

The 1938 League Champions, known as the "Jacobus Reserve" included Dallas Darr, P. Brownie, Leroy "Fatty" Myers, Earl "Easter" Hildebrand, Erwin "Buzzard" Shearer, Pat Innerst, Dub McDonald, Lieb McDonald, Norman "Bud" Shearer, Milt Diehl, Clair Trout, Bud King, Merlin "Speck" Myers, Muggs Forry (Manager), Bill Hildebrand (Scorekeeper). Herb Geiselman is not on the picture.

This photo was taken from an article in the York Dispatch Newspaper published on June 11, 1987. It appeared as part of a Jacobus sesquicentennial news article.

The Jacobus Ball Team and field – 1938. York Road runs left to right behind the dugout. (Photo courtesy of Sylvia Yarnell (Myers))

The Jacobus Ball Team and field – 1938. The home in the background belonged to Leroy "Fatty" Myers, one of the Jacobus Players. (Photo courtesy of Sylvia Yarnell (Myers))

The Jacobus Ball field – 1938. Facing home plate, backstop, and spectators. Pretty amazing flag pole! (Photo courtesy of Sylvia Yarnell (Myers))

Back in Business

It's a beautiful day for baseball.

— Ernie Banks

1946 – 1947 Seasons

At the end of World War II, in 1946, baseball is revived again in Jacobus. The community has built a new ballfield at the Ollie Hess farm at the north end of town. My uncle Bob remembers, "After the guys came back from the war, Paul Smith was one of the primary guys... Paul Smith was one of the people that put together the team after the war."

The new field is located at a lot on the corner of Main Street (Route 111) and Geiselman Drive, which runs west off of Route 111 at the north end of town. Home plate and the backstop are located at the southwest corner of the property. The Ollie Hess property is used to play baseball during the 1946 and 1947 seasons. The Jacobus team is competing in the Greater York County League at this time.

The only other places in town to play ball, are a property on Water Street named Lakeview Park, owned by the Evangelical Church, and the playground at the school house at the south end of town. The Church property and the school property are too small for real baseball fields, so they are only used informally to play ball and to practice. The Ollie Hess farm however provides plenty of room. Left, center, and right fields at this property have long distances to be covered.

Although this field is the best available, the condition of the field is not always the best. There are no mowers available for the team to mow the outfield grass, other than hay mowers. At times the ball gets lost in the outfield. "One time I saw a fielder roll in the grass to find the ball," my uncle Lee Arnold recalls. As noted, the field is not in the best condition some of the time, but no one seems to mind that much.

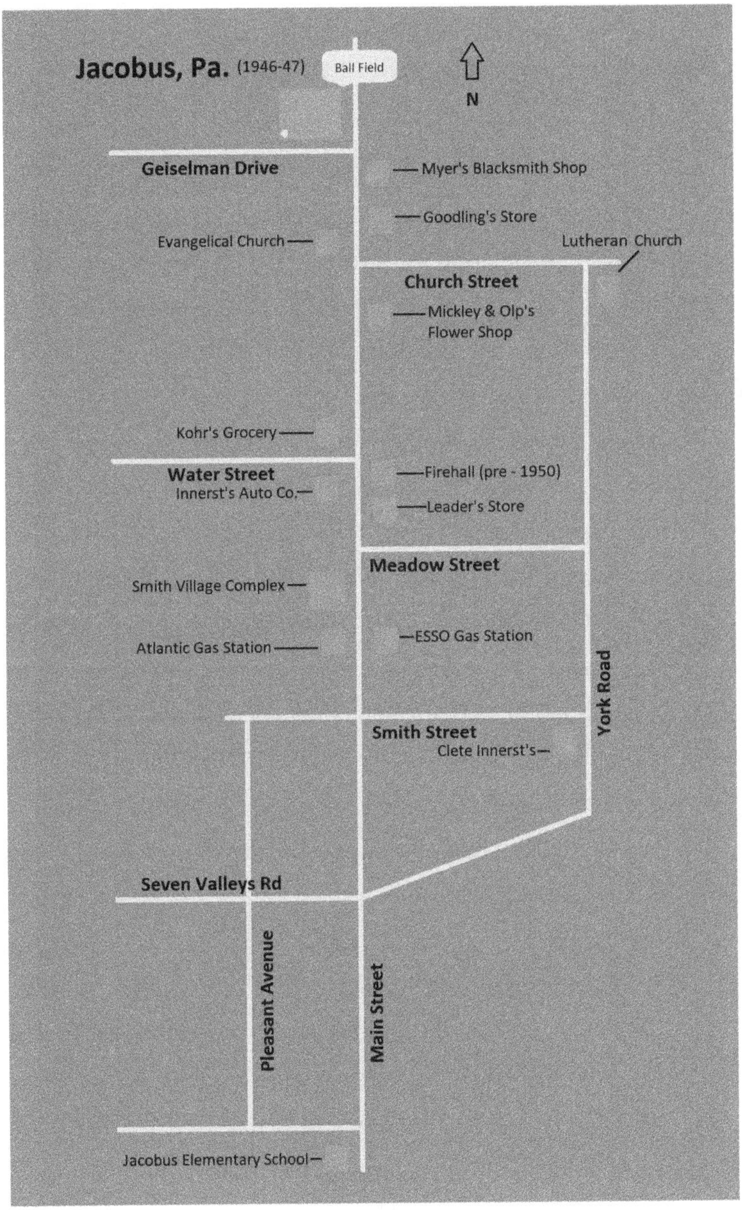
Jacobus, Pa. (1946-47)
Ball Field
N
Geiselman Drive
Myer's Blacksmith Shop
Goodling's Store
Evangelical Church
Lutheran Church
Church Street
Mickley & Olp's
Flower Shop
Kohr's Grocery
Water Street
Innerst's Auto Co.
Firehall (pre - 1950)
Leader's Store
Meadow Street
Smith Village Complex
ESSO Gas Station
Atlantic Gas Station
York Road
Smith Street
Clete Innerst's
Seven Valleys Rd
Pleasant Avenue
Main Street
Jacobus Elementary School

I asked my Dad about the popularity of baseball at that time. He said, "Well, basically baseball was a big thing back then. A lot bigger than it is today. We have some baseball fans today, but baseball was a pretty big event back in those days. There were baseball teams all over the county; more than what they have right now. Anybody that wanted to play showed up, and if they had enough uniforms you got a uniform. They never kicked anybody off of a team. Your ability determined whether you played or not because of the large number of players who came out to play. Eventually, we added a second team – to give more people a chance to play. At that time, I was around seventeen or eighteen years old. Some players were older and some younger than that." Dad added a little more about some of the players, "I was a catcher, played the outfield, and I pitched one game when I was manager of the second team. On the second team that I managed later in the forties, Roy Warfel was the fast ball pitcher. Shrummy (Gerald Schrum) was a curveball pitcher on the second team. The first team had Whitey Allison. He was a fastball pitcher. And then there was Mooney Allison. He was a big fastball pitcher. They played on the big (first) team, and Heinie Heltzel, who was a major league player at one time, played shortstop for the big team." (Author's note – This would have been after Heinie's professional career.) "Carroll Hildebrand umpired. They probably got five dollars a game to umpire. They used to give the pitchers a couple of dollars a game also. Pret Hershner coached the second team for the first couple of years. I coached the second team for a couple of years. Bud Shearer, I think, was a manager of the first team, but there was somebody else before him. I can't think of who that was."

The baseball teams of this time almost always provide a good caliber of baseball and attract nice sized crowds. To reinforce that point, the Jacobus team is Greater York County League champs in 1947. There are championship trophies, and patches given out, and a banquet held as a part of the celebration for a tremendous season. Vic Wertz, who is a professional ball player with the Detroit Tigers and who was born in nearby York, PA., is a featured speaker at the banquet.

The ball field at the Ollie Hess farm is only used for two seasons. The 1947 season is the last season that will be played there. Down the road a number of years, a fairly large manufacturing building will be built on this farm property. A number of different companies will occupy the space, including Merry Mites clothing and AMP Incorporated electronics.

The 1947 Baseball Team – (Back row L-R) Carl (Bud) Smith, Clarke (Jake) Shearer, Ralph (Pally) Innerst, Paul (Jake) Smith, Pret Hershner. (Front row L-R) Bill Shearer, Don (Pepper) Rohrbaugh, Jesse (Jet) Keeney, Carl (Red) Arnold, Bob Falkenstine, Karl Folkenroth, Rich Arnold. (Up front) Jay Snyder. Photo taken at the Ollie Hess Farm field. (Photo courtesy of Carl "Red" Arnold)

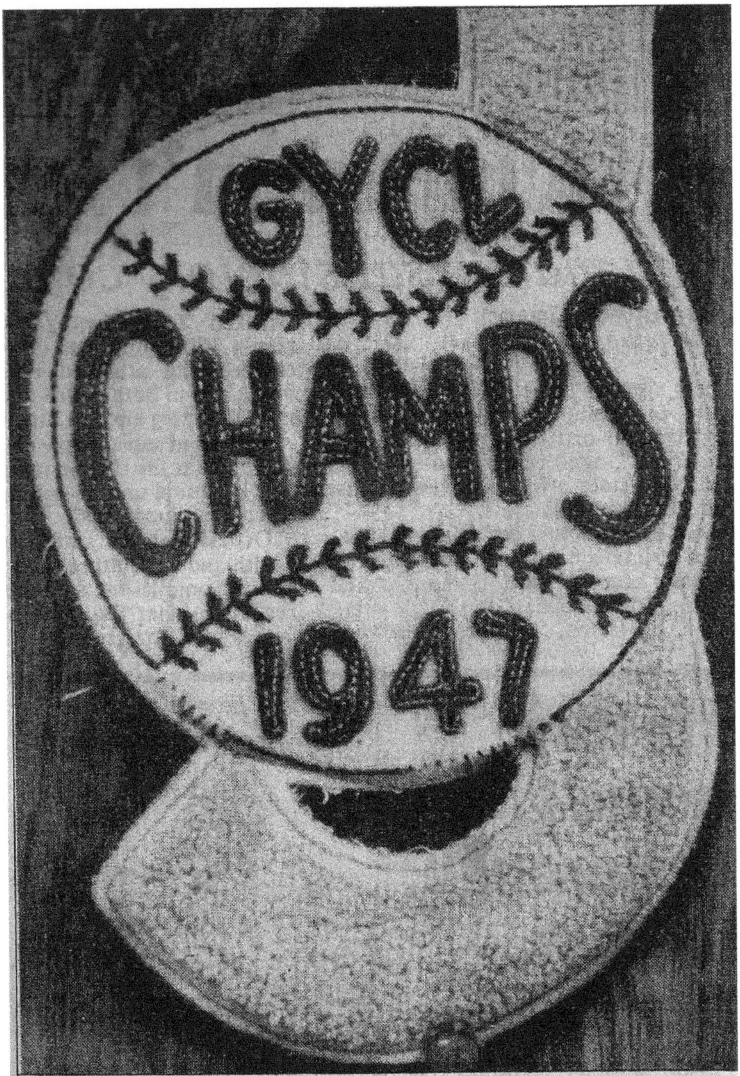

A memento of the Greater York County League, circa 1947.

1947 Greater York County League Champions - patch. (York Daily Record Newspaper, Jacobus sesquicentennial coverage, May 30, 1987)

1947 Greater York County League Champions – Jacobus Athletic Association Trophy.

1947 Greater York County League Champions. (Back row L – R) Business Manager - Carroll Hildebrand, Paul Smith, Pret Hershner, Perry Innerst Jr., Clarke Shearer, Earl Hildebrand, Carl Bud Smith, Russell Shearer Sr., Manager – Ralph Pallie Innerst. (First row L – R) Carl Red Arnold, Donald Rohrbaugh, Carl Folkenroth, Jesse Keeney, Bob Falkenstine, Richard Arnold, William Shearer.(Front row) Jay Snyder. (Photo taken at the Jacobus school house.)

Autograph of Vic Wertz in the bottom right corner – he was a major league player at that time with the Detroit Tigers –Mr. Wertz was a speaker at the Jacobus Ball Team's banquet. (Photo by Larry Stump, October 5, 1947) (Photo courtesy of Carl "Red" Arnold)

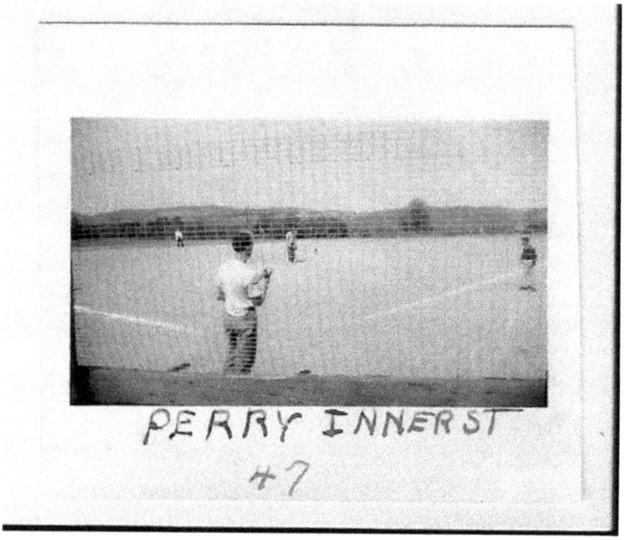

Perry Innerst at the plate during practice - Photo taken at the Ollie Hess Farm field. (Photo courtesy of Carl "Red" Arnold)

High Jinks in Town and other Stories

I took a little English, a little math, some science, a few hubcaps, and some wheel covers.

— Outfielder Gates Brown on his high school years

1940s

Since these chapters discuss the actions mostly of teenagers and those in their early 20s, it goes without saying that besides playing baseball and working for local farms and businesses, there were some shenanigans going on at times. Here are some stories from my uncles Bob and Lee and my mom and dad.

A different world – (From my uncle Bob) – "And one thing to give you an idea of the times… When I was in eighth grade we were playing hide-and-seek, and we had snow fences up yet, and they were held in place by guide wires. I was running down… running from home base at the school and hit one of those wires and tore my lip open. And it knocked me down and stung me, and I see I'm bleeding. So, I went into the school. And I still remember Homer Geiselman (Author – Homer. Geiselman was the school teacher.) saying, "It looks like that's going to take stitches". I had no idea what stiches were. Now, they sent me, Gordy Rehmeyer, and Gene Snyder walking home… I walked home with a handkerchief held in my face to stop the bleeding. We lived in Jacobus yet at that time. They stayed with a couple of my younger brothers who were still at home, and Mom took me up to Doc Krout to get my lip sewn up. And I can remember… this was toward the end his career… and I can still see his hand shaking while he was trying to sew me up. And he said - I'll never forget it - "you won't see the stitches by the time you get married". Well, I can still see them and that's about fifty years later. But the signs of the time are… that they didn't even drive me home. I walked home from the school holding a handkerchief to stop the bleeding. Can you imagine what would happen today if something like that happened? They'd have the police, the fire engine, the ambulance. There would be lawsuits. That's just the way things were then."

Cart on the Barber Shop roof – Uncle Lee: "Then there was kind of a cart that was put on top of the barbershop…"

Uncle Bob: “And this same cart… I would have been a junior or senior in high school… The cart was moved one time to where the original Ollie Hess Farm ball diamond was, where the AMP building is now… and a big sign was placed on it “Brown's Modern Bus Service”. A guy by the name of Brown owned a bus service that transported us to school in the morning and then brought us home in the evening and he was kind of a cranky guy. So, he was… he did not appreciate that this buggy was set along the road with a big sign on for Brown's Modern Bus Service.

Halloween – (From my uncle Lee) – “I’ll tell you… Halloween lasted about two weeks before Halloween. You know soaping windows and….

Uncle Bob chimes in: “Carrying furniture off…”

Uncle Lee: “They’d burn corn fodder shocks… Frank Smith’s farm would provide that… you know after you husked the corn you have it shocked up there and some of the older guys, I don't know who they were, but they would burn corn fodder shocks.”

Uncle Bob: “We had no police around at that time. The state police did all the monitoring. Soaping at N.J. Leaders…you know the big display windows at his place…that was a big thing… soaping windows, throwing shelled corn on porches and things like that. You’d go through town days before

Halloween… dressed up in clothing so people wouldn't know who you were… did your Dad tell you that?"

The Jacobus Comfort Station – Uncle Bob: "One Halloween, Clete Innerest had an outhouse down at his place. You know where Clete Innerst's was? Down close to where Bruce's (Smith Village) place is. He had an outhouse there. This outhouse was carried up to the square of Jacobus, up where Kohr's store was at Water Street. And the next morning for everyone to see, there was a sign on it that said "Jacobus Comfort Station".

Car in the elementary school – Uncle Bob: "Did your Dad tell you the story about how he stayed out of trouble… because we were in at the Deitz farm one Sunday evening… and his buddies broke into the school and pushed that old car that was floating around town into the hallway of the elementary school? Red would have been with them if we would not have been in on the farm. Yeah, but because Louie Stough's Dad was chairman of the school board nothing ever came of it. But they opened…. got the doors to the school opened on the back side and pushed this car into the hall. This was the Jacobus school, out there at the ball diamond."

(Author) I gave my Dad a chance to deny any participation in these events… Dad: "I was never involved with the wagon or buggy on top of the barber shop, but I did help to roll toilets over. We would just lay them back. That was Halloween. We got our heads dunked on with water over at N.J. Leaders one time. We started to soap his big windows and he was upstairs… he went upstairs and dumped water on us."

Scrap metal for the war and paper drives – (From my uncle Bob) – "Another thing, during World War II there was a scrap drive. And in front of Kohr's store (Author – Located at the corner of Main and Water streets.) …you know it was a kind of a large area there... the people from the surrounding area there in the town were encouraged to bring any kind of scrap iron for the war effort. And it tended to be an accumulation of all kinds of miscellaneous scrap iron stuff in that pile."

Uncle Lee also reminded me about the paper drives that the Boy Scouts did. They went door-to-door around the town collecting old newspapers. Scrap paper was put to a number of different uses during the war.

Women's Involvement – (Author - I asked my Mom about what the women were up to at the time, related to what was going on with the Athletic Association and baseball… "Did you do anything… help organize or sell anything, etc.?") Mom: "We weren't really involved directly. Many of the women who had kids just stayed home to take care of them. We just cheered and fought the other fans. If they were playing Lincoln Way, everybody yelled like crazy and oh my gosh… fans from Lincoln Way were so nasty and would come out onto the field. Lots of stuff like that. None of the women played ball. It was strictly a guys' thing. We just went to the games to see your team win."

Mom does remember however, some guy, who possibly played on a West York Team, called "Snowball". Evidently this guy had a lot of lady fans. Anyway... "We just watched the guys. That's as good as it got."

(Author - Although it's not mentioned in the Association minutes, my Mom typed up the original copy of the Association Bylaws, which are shown in the Appendix B. It appears that women never attended the Athletic Association meetings, however as the times changed, women did eventually begin to get involved later in the Jacobus Recreation Association.)

Strawberry Fields

Ballparks should be happy places. They should always smell like freshly cut grass.

— Team owner Bill Veek

Late 1947

At the end of the 1947 season, after discussions with the Jacobus Baseball Team and the Community it was decided to buy a piece of property, located at the south end of Jacobus, from Mont Smith.

Mont Smith was a farmer who owned a lot of property on the south and west sides of Jacobus. His crops were mostly strawberries and beans. Unlike many of the other area farmers, he didn't raise cattle or grow a lot of corn. The Mont Smith house was located on the west side of Jacobus along what is now Smith Street.

Strawberries are not the sweetest fruit and picking them, not the easiest job. Bending over all day to pick strawberries might make you wish that you were picking apples or cherries instead. Anyway, it's not the easiest work, but it paid as well as anything else a teenager could get.

Here's a little bit about the strawberry business back then, as described by my Dad... "Picking strawberries depends on you, and on how fast you go, because you get paid by the box. You usually start about nine o'clock in the morning because things have to be dried off to pick. You work until 4 PM many times. You take your strawberries to a certain station to get registered and then get another set of boxes. There are around eight or so boxes to a carrier.

Strawberry season usually begins in late May and lasts a few weeks into June. Mont Smith's sons, Jake and Bud Smith, were the supervisors. Sometimes some on the work crew would deliver strawberries up to the Hershey Ice Cream facility near Harrisburg, PA. The crew would take loads of strawberries in a box truck. The nights were spent up in the nearby mountain areas in a cabin owned by either Nevin Smith or Bruce Smith, then the crew would come back and work the next day. The crew delivered fifty crates or more of strawberries each delivery" .

The piece of Mont Smith's property that the Jacobus Baseball Team wanted to purchase was between Pleasant Avenue and Franklin Street, off of what will later be called School Road. This was part of the farm which had provided great strawberries and other vegetables over the years. Although Mont Smith was starting to reduce the amount of farming he was involved with at this time, there was still plenty of ground remaining, even after selling this property.

The property was informally purchased by the Jacobus Baseball Team at the end of 1947, although no deed had yet been transferred. The official record of the exact purchase price from this transaction cannot be located, but my uncle Bob Arnold and Richard Bupp, who both were involved with the team at the time, agree that the total purchase price was around $3000.

There were a few businessmen in the community, including Sam Babble and Nevin Smith, who helped the team financially in many ways. As is noted in the records of the Jacobus Athletic Association, it appeared that around $2000 of the total was paid as a down payment. Some of the funds came out of the Jacobus Baseball Team's funds and some came as loans from the community's businessmen.

The actual transfer of the deed from Mont Smith to the Jacobus Athletic Association took place on July 7, 1949 for the amount of $1. On June 24, 1953 the property on the other side of Pleasant Avenue, which eventually became the playground and recreation area, was purchased. The addition of this second property almost doubled the size of the original property. On June 30, 1959 the property was transferred from the Jacobus Athletic Association to the Jacobus Borough for the amount of $1. Included in this deed was a clause to guarantee the legacy - "...to the condition which is made part of the consideration for this conveyance, that the land herby granted shall always be used as a public playground and shall not be used for any other purpose...". In the Appendix of this book are a lot more details about the purchase of the property, including copies of the deeds.

The purchase in 1947 was the first step of many to follow, leading to something down the road which no one would have imagined at that time.

The Jacobus Athletic Association

Give a boy a bat and a ball and a place to play and you'll have a good citizen.

— Hall of Famer Joe McCarthy

Late 1947 – Early 1948

While arrangements are going on to purchase the piece of property for the new ball field, something else is going on that will provide a solid foundation for everything else that follows. The **Jacobus Athletic Association** is formed in December 1947 as a non-profit organization.

According to my Dad, "We were just a baseball team club, and depending on what you were doing, you had to be declared a charity organization. Otherwise you would be paying more taxes on fundraising income. That's why we formed an official organization, and it was certified by the Court of Common Pleas, or something like that." …

The first meeting of the Jacobus Athletic Association is held in the basement of Clete Innerst's business on December 11th, 1947. This building is located on the corner of York Road and Smith Street, near the location of the old 1938 baseball diamond. This also becomes the location of many of the meetings that follow. My Dad mentioned, "Except for an addition in the back since then, the building is pretty much the same as it was back in 1947."

At the time of this first Association meeting my Dad is 18 years old and had just graduated from high school. Many of the founding members are just out of high school and are in their late teens or early twenties.

Individuals mentioned in the minutes from that first Association meeting are: Ralph Innerst, Preston Hershner, Nevin Smith, Sidney Straley, Richard Arnold, Carl Folkenroth, Earl Hildebrand, Allan Falkenstine, C. L. Innerst, Howard Olp, Elmer Geiselman, W. H. Hildebrand, Karl Smith, Kenneth Keiser, Carroll Hildebrand, Paul Smith, Donald Rohrbaugh, and Carl D. Arnold.

The first group of elected officers are; Election Board – Ken Keiser, Don Rohrbaugh, and Carl "Red" Arnold President - Ralph Innerst, Vice President – Preston Hershner, Secretary – Sid Straley, Assistant Secretary – Rich Arnold,

Treasurer – Nevin Smith, Business Managers – Carroll Hildebrand and Paul Smith. Others involved in the election are Carl Folkenroth and Earl Hildebrand. The first elected Board of Directors are: A. P. Falkenstine, C. L. Innerst, Howard Olp, Elmer Geiselman, and Nevin Smith.

In this first meeting of the Association a motion is made to make a payment to Nevin Smith of $280 to cover part of his payment for the new field. Things are already in-motion regarding the new field, as another motion is made at this meeting to have C. L. Innerst grade the new field as soon as possible.

Looking ahead, this meeting is the first in a series of regular monthly meetings held over the next ten years or so, where gradually all of the pieces will come together and all of the decisions will be made. The end result in the upcoming years will be the creation of a baseball diamond and recreation park, which will appear out of what was at one time a farmer's strawberry field.

Following are some excerpts from the Association minutes of 1948. (I'm paraphrasing.)

As of January 6, 1948, all of the assets of the Jacobus Baseball Team amount to $520.04. This amount is then turned over to the Jacobus Athletic Association. The Jacobus Baseball Team already had some assets because you had to pay the umpires, buy baseballs and uniforms and all of that kind of thing.

Some of the businesses in town also contribute funds to the cause.

In February 1948, Ralph Innerst is appointed Manager of the baseball team for 1948. A full constitution and By-Laws are adopted stating the name of the new organization is the "Jacobus Athletic Association". The membership fee to join the Association is $2.00. Dues are $1.00 per year. Those under 16 can join the Association but only those 16 and above are able to cast votes in elections or on whatever topics come up for a vote. A motion is made and approved to begin building bleachers and other spectator and player facilities as needed. W. H. Hildebrand is nominated for and accepted, "with some hesitation", the position of first grounds keeper of the new field. Other member's in attendance at this meeting, other than the Officers, are Clair Smith, Harry Keiser, Sterling Myers, Caleb Ferree, Herb Geiselman, Arthur Shearer, and Clarke Shearer. On March 30, 1948 Nevin Smith reported the estimate to build bleachers will be around $600.00.

In 1948 Jacobus has one team in the Greater York County League. It is decided that a "second team" will be added which will be in the newly formed Western Baseball League. Preston Hershner is named manager of the second team. Members of that first "second team" include Perry Innerst, Jr., Clarke Shearer, Richard Bupp, Bob Falkenstine, Lee Arnold, Vernon Geiselman, Carl "Red" Arnold, Amos Warfel, Rich Arnold, Gerry Snyder, Gerald Schrum, Roy Warfel, Charlie Smith, and Dale Innerst. Steve Hershner is designated as bat boy. (There is a more detailed discussion of the different teams and leagues in

Appendix C.). An appeal is made at the meeting for all members to turn out to help get the new field in shape for the coming season.

At the Association meeting on April 27, 1948, it is approved to borrow $500.00 to pay bills contracted in connection with the construction of the bleachers. One of the fund-raising activities includes selling spaces on the game scorecards. It is reported that so far $362.50 has been made selling space on the scorecards.

Here is a description from my Dad about how the construction of the ball field took place; "Clete Innerst and Palley (Ralph) Innerst graded the field. We really didn't do too much to it. The land was pretty much the way it was. We did take some of the ground down toward School Road to level the infield off a little bit. Right field still went up a slope a little bit, though not a whole lot. Left field went downhill a little bit. We put in a backstop. The pipes for the back stop were supplied by Jacobus Plastics, Inc., courtesy of Ben Franklin. Cement block bleachers were built on the first base and third base sides of the field. Ed Ferree, who lived out on Lake Road, was a mason/block layer and directed the building of the bleachers and dugouts. (Author - Lake Road is about a mile to the east of Jacobus.) Some of us mixed mortar and helped carry the blocks to get them into position. Then we put wooden seats on the bleachers. We had a wooden backstop about four feet high and then the rest of it was wire fence. We put up dugouts on the first and third base sides. All of the guys helped to build them. It was a grass infield from the start, with ground for the base lines and the infield. I think that we only did grass seed on the infield and back a little bit because the outfield was just kind of graded and that was not a regular lawn seed planted there… kind of like a hay seed you might say. We eventually put up a small block house behind the backstop for concession sales, but at first, the concession stand was just an outdoor thing."

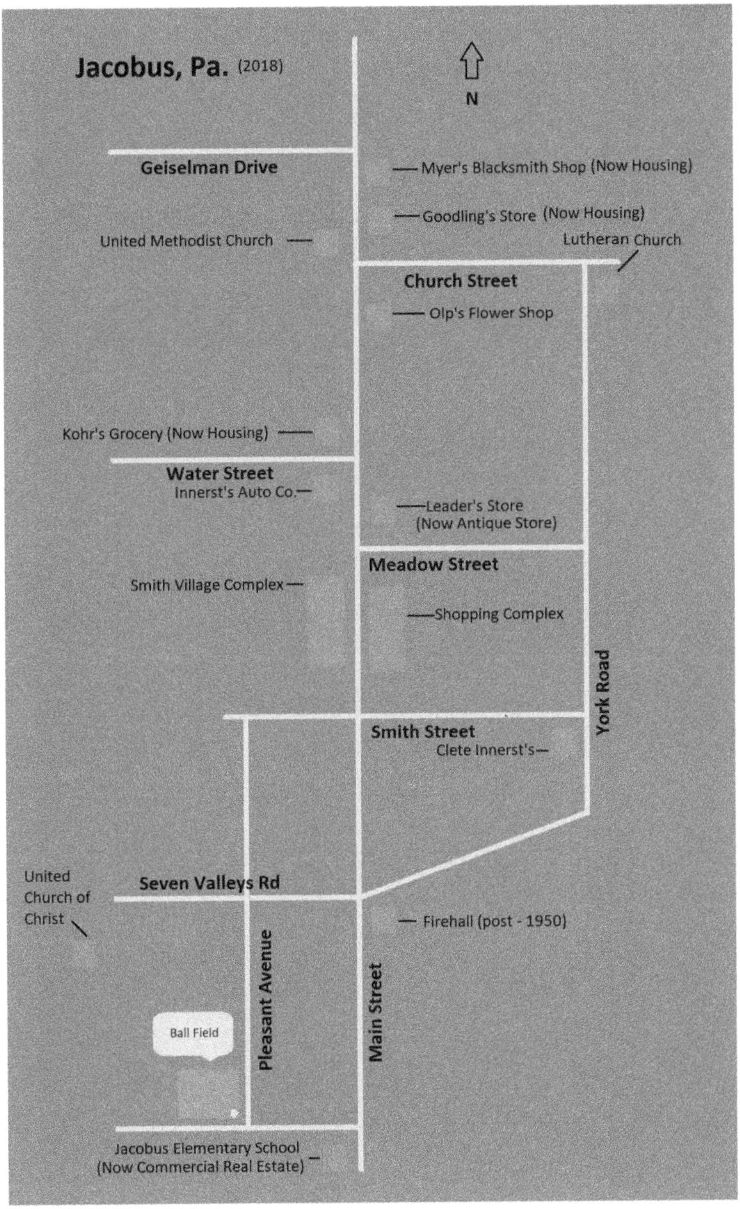
Jacobus, Pa. (2018)
N
Geiselman Drive
Myer's Blacksmith Shop (Now Housing)
Goodling's Store (Now Housing)
United Methodist Church
Lutheran Church
Church Street
Olp's Flower Shop
Kohr's Grocery (Now Housing)
Water Street
Innerst's Auto Co.
Leader's Store
(Now Antique Store)
Meadow Street
Smith Village Complex
Shopping Complex
York Road
Smith Street
Clete Innerst's
United
Church of
Christ
Seven Valleys Rd
Firehall (post - 1950)
Pleasant Avenue
Main Street
Ball Field
Jacobus Elementary School
(Now Commercial Real Estate)

By the spring of 1949 the membership of the Jacobus Athletic Association has grown to around 144. For those interested in the "play-by-play" description of Association meetings through the years, Appendix B. contains a lot of the details, taken from the recorded minutes of the Jacobus Athletic Association.

Play Ball!

In the beginning there was a word and the word was "Play Ball".
— Writer George Bowering

Spring 1948

In May of 1948 it is now time to start the new baseball season at the new baseball park. At the May 25th, 1948 Jacobus Athletic Association meeting, a committee is appointed to arrange for a dedication ceremony for the new field. Appointed to serve on this committee are Bill Hildebrand, A. P. Falkenstine, and Elmer Geiselman. The dedication ceremony is to take place at the first game of the season. (Note that this committee was appointed only 4 days before the ceremony was to take place!) At the Association meeting there are discussions about field equipment that still needs to be procured – a batter's screen for batting practice, a scoreboard, and forms for chalk-lining the batter's box and coaches' boxes.

The new field is dedicated on **Saturday May 29th, 1948**. There is a band composed of local musicians which provides music for the flag raising and opening ceremony. A talk is given during the opening ceremony by H. J. Geiselman, a Jacobus school teacher. Last but not least, Burgess Dr. G. Elmer Krout throws out the first ball at the game to get things started. Following this dedication, the first game at the new field is a Greater League game with Stoverstown.

On that Saturday in May I doubt that many there knew that this was the beginning of something that would become a source of great pride for the community on into the next century. And just in case you missed it, one of the main points that the author has tried to make clear in this story so far, is that this baseball field, and the recreation complex that will follow in the upcoming years, came into being due to the efforts of the community coming together to supply 100% of the planning, skills, labor, and funds that it took to make it happen. No small feat when you think about it.

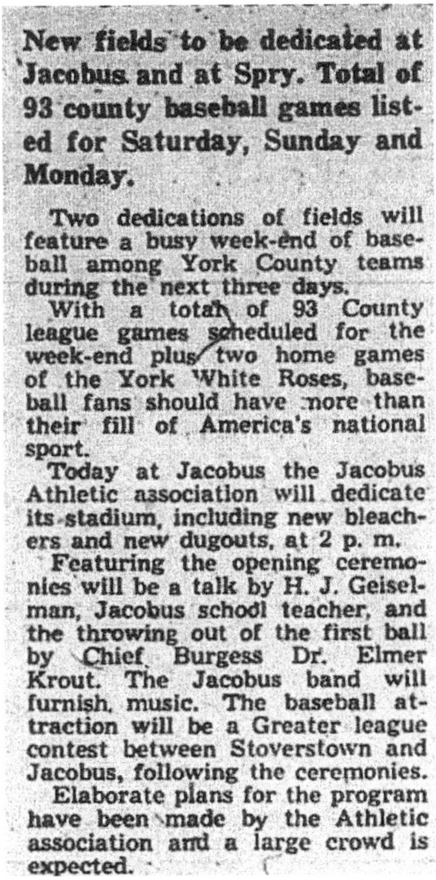

New fields to be dedicated at Jacobus and at Spry. Total of 93 county baseball games listed for Saturday, Sunday and Monday.

Two dedications of fields will feature a busy week-end of baseball among York County teams during the next three days.

With a total of 93 County league games scheduled for the week-end plus two home games of the York White Roses, baseball fans should have more than their fill of America's national sport.

Today at Jacobus the Jacobus Athletic association will dedicate its stadium, including new bleachers and new dugouts, at 2 p. m.

Featuring the opening ceremonies will be a talk by H. J. Geiselman, Jacobus school teacher, and the throwing out of the first ball by Chief Burgess Dr. Elmer Krout. The Jacobus band will furnish music. The baseball attraction will be a Greater league contest between Stoverstown and Jacobus, following the ceremonies.

Elaborate plans for the program have been made by the Athletic association and a large crowd is expected.

Portion of an article appearing in the York Gazette and Daily Newspaper on May 29th, 1948, describing the dedication ceremony. (Courtesy of York Heritage Trust Library/Archives)

Raising the flag in center field, accompanied by the local band. Opening Day, field dedication May 29th, 1948. (Photo courtesy of Carl "Red" Arnold)

Dedication ceremony in center field. Opening Day, field dedication May 29th, 1948. (Photo courtesy of Carl "Red" Arnold)

Another view of the dedication ceremony in center field. Opening Day, field dedication May 29th, 1948. (Photo courtesy of Carl "Red" Arnold)

First pitch by Dr. Krout. Opening Day, field dedication May 29th, 1948. (Photo courtesy of Carl "Red" Arnold)

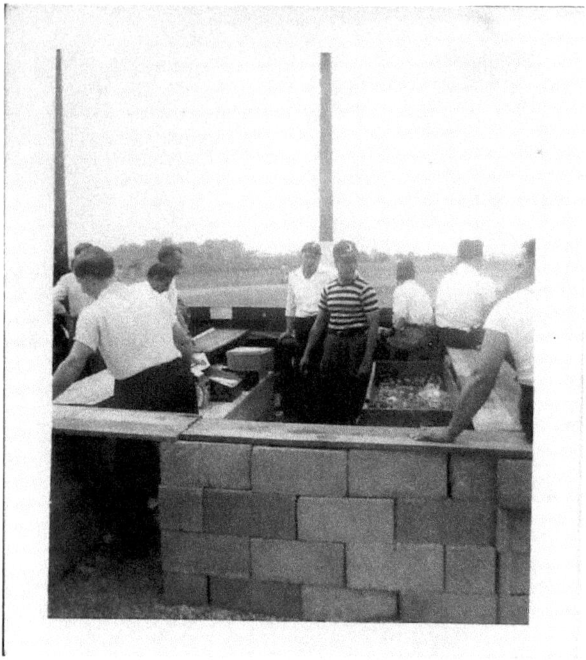

Concession sales behind the backstop. My Dad's on the left with his back to the camera, helping to assemble the concession stand. Also, on concession stand duty are John Schroll and George "Juice" Keeney (L – R). Opening Day, May 29th, 1948. (Photo courtesy of Carl "Red" Arnold)

Some action down the first base line. Opening Day, May 29th, 1948. (Photo courtesy of Carl "Red" Arnold)

Jake Smith delivering to the plate. Opening Day, May 29th, 1948. (Photo courtesy of Carl "Red" Arnold)

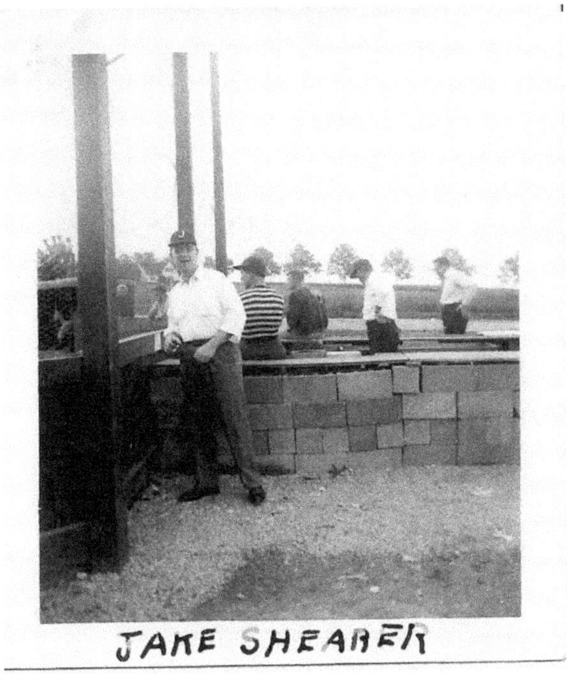

Jake Shearer behind the backstop. Opening Day, May 29th, 1948. (Photo courtesy of Carl "Red" Arnold)

The visitors side bleachers. Opening Day, May 29th, 1948. (Photo courtesy of Carl "Red" Arnold)

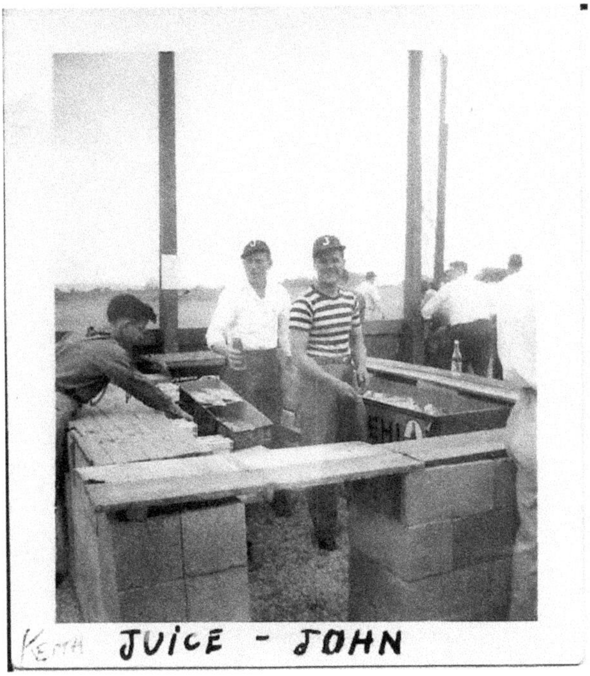

John Schroll and George "Juice" Keeney manning the concession stand (L – R). Opening Day, May 29th, 1948. (Photo courtesy of Carl "Red" Arnold)

Leroy Myers, umpire behind the plate. Opening Day, May 29th, 1948. (Photo courtesy of Carl "Red" Arnold)

Home team dugout and bleachers. Opening Day, May 29th, 1948. (Photo courtesy of Carl "Red" Arnold)

Russ Shearer at first. Opening Day, May 29th, 1948. (Photo courtesy of Carl "Red" Arnold)

View of the infield from the third base side. Opening Day, May 29th, 1948. (Photo courtesy of Carl "Red" Arnold)

Building the Legacy

Every day is a new opportunity. You can build on yesterday's success or put its failures behind and start over again. That's the way life is, with a new game every day, and that's the way baseball is.

— Hall of Famer Bob Feller, from *Baseball and the Meaning of Life*, edited by Josh Leventhal

Late 1940's through 1959

1948 - Back then there was great community interest in local baseball. My uncle Lee's observations - "The games were well attended with 400 to 500 fans. Some county games would have a thousand fans attending. We played Tuesday and Thursday evenings and Saturday afternoons. On Memorial Day and July Fourth, we played a morning and afternoon game. One at home and one away. At that time there were still the 'Blue Laws' in the state which didn't allow games to be played on Sundays.

But then sometime in the fifties some teams started to play on Sundays and before long, all teams played make-up games at times on Sunday. There were some players that didn't play because of religious beliefs. In those days, most families didn't take vacations and this was a primary entertainment for families. They followed the teams to away games."

In December of 1948 after a year in the books for the new ball park, the decision is made to purchase 35 feet to increase the baseball field from right field to center fields. This is additional property was owned by Mont Smith. The cost is $280.00.

At this point it's around 333 ft. down the left field line, 325 ft. down the right field line, and around 465 ft. to the far corner of center field.

There are no homes directly beyond right and right-center fields yet, although there are a few further north along Pleasant Avenue. There are no homes yet directly beyond left field, but it won't be long before two homes are constructed on that side of the field also. Sol Decker's home will be built not too far beyond left field, and at the far end of the left field line there is a 157 ft. by 60 ft. lot that indents into the left field line corner of the property. This is will soon have a home built and owned by Jack Meyers.

As mentioned, there is a lot of interest in baseball in the county. There are enough teams to fill a number of different leagues. Some of the leagues are the **Greater York County League**, the **Southern York County League**, the **Twilight League**, the **Western League**, the **City-County League**, and the **Central York County League**. (Details of which leagues the Jacobus teams played in are detailed in Appendix C.)

In 1948, in addition to the primary team, Jacobus decides to form a "second" team. This team has younger players and is composed of mostly high school kids or kids one or two years out of high school. The second team is allowed to have two players over twenty-one.

1949 - With a shiny new baseball park up and running for a year, 1949 continues the tradition of baseball in Jacobus. In 1949 Jacobus starts a 13 to 15 Baseball for Boys' team. The town's kids in this age bracket now have an organized team to play on. Prior to this, the kids would play pick-up teams from neighboring towns. Since there were so few guys with cars, some even walked to the games. The Baseball for Boys team can now play other teams in the county just like the "first" and "second" teams have been doing.

In the fall of 1949 the Jacobus second team is in a championship playoff at the York Memorial Stadium. This is the home stadium used by the minor league "York White Roses" team, so this is a big deal for the players. During the playoff's Jacobus beats the York Crispus Attucks team to win the playoffs.

City County League Playoff Winners – 1949 Front row: Gerald Schrum, Steve Hershner, Roy Warfel. 2nd Row: Vernon Geiselman, Red Arnold, Amos Warfel, Richard Arnold, Gerry Snyder. 3rd row: Pret Hershner, Perry Innerst, Clarke Shearer, Richard Bupp, Bob Falkenstine, Lee Arnold. (Photo courtesy of Carl "Red" Arnold)

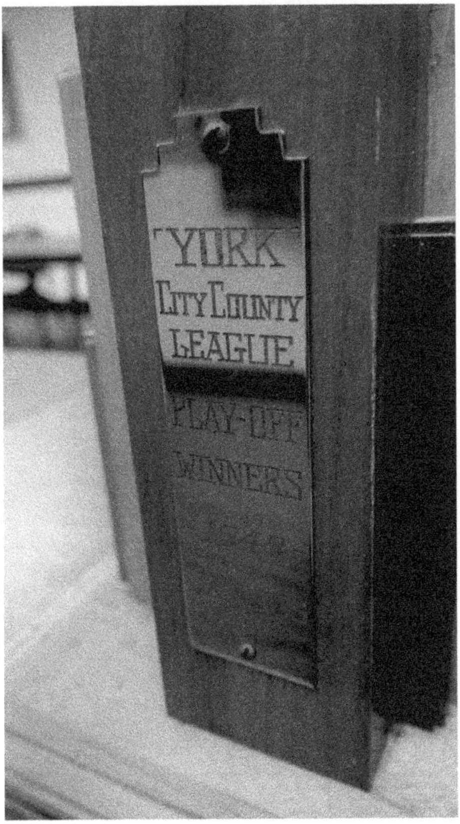

City County League Playoff Winners Trophy – 1949

City County League Playoff Winners Trophy – 1949

No one is sure exactly when it started in the county leagues, but in some cases, things were taking on a more "professional" feel with some of the local teams. Besides players, umpires were also paid for their labors. Some pitchers were being paid $2 or $3 per game. Here's a description about this from my uncle Ted. (This description appears in context in Appendix C. – Teams and Leagues.)

"Red Lion, would load up their team with guys from all over the county. There was a guy from Red Lion... I don't know what his first name was... his last name was Horn. And he had money. In fact, their baseball diamond and also a football stadium were named after the family.... Red Lion stadium... I mean it had a big fence all the way around the outfield you know... And he would pay. Back then they had people that would pay for guys to come and play for them. And they were really good. Horn was good and he had the money... he was a big guy. He played first base."

"Jacobus didn't have too many paid players. I tell you most of the Jacobus team was local. Most of them were local. There was a guy named Les Williams. (Author - My uncle may have meant Les Lehman, who is someone mentioned in the Athletic Association minutes as causing some complaints at one meeting because of his price.) He came in and he managed for a couple years. And I kind of think he might have got paid because he was from another town. He was from Red Lion or Felton."

"And then there was a guy from York... Stagemyer? his name was. He was a pitcher and he pitched for us. And then we would get some kids from... well... some kids from college, that went to York College. In the summer they were looking for teams to play on and we had a couple... in fact two of them... Your Dad might remember these. Don Loucks was one of them... there were two of them that came out and inquired about whether they'd be able to play baseball with us. Don Loucks was one of them and I forget what the other guy's name was. So, they played a couple of years with Jacobus. And then there was one or two other guys too that I remember coming from York and playing out here."

At the end of 1949, a group of Jacobus boys formed a basketball team. Here's some information on the Jacobus Basketball team, courtesy of my uncle Lee - "When I was around 15 we formed a town basketball team. We played any team we could find to play against. It was mostly against other town teams and church teams in York. We were not in a league but played an independent schedule. We rented the Seven Valleys Fire Hall floor to practice and play our games. When Jacobus built a new Fire Hall we lobbied to have a basketball floor put in but didn't get it. After it was built we convinced them to let us put up baskets in the auditorium so that we could practice. It had a ceiling only about 15 feet high, but we eventually played some games in it. We bought uniforms ourselves that were green and white. I usually played guard." The team included Richard Bupp, Richard Arnold, Lee Arnold, Gerry Snyder, Gene Snyder, Ray Shearer, Jr., Bob Falkenstine, Larry Smith and Danny Smith.

The Jacobus Basketball Team – Formed in 1949. Front row: Richard Arnold, Jay Snyder, Marvin (Lee) Arnold, Robert Falkenstine. Back row: Gene Snyder, Larry Smith, Gerald Snyder, Richard Bupp, Dale Innerst. (Photo courtesy of Carl "Red" Arnold)

1950 - In 1950, new baseball uniforms were purchased to supplement those already being used.

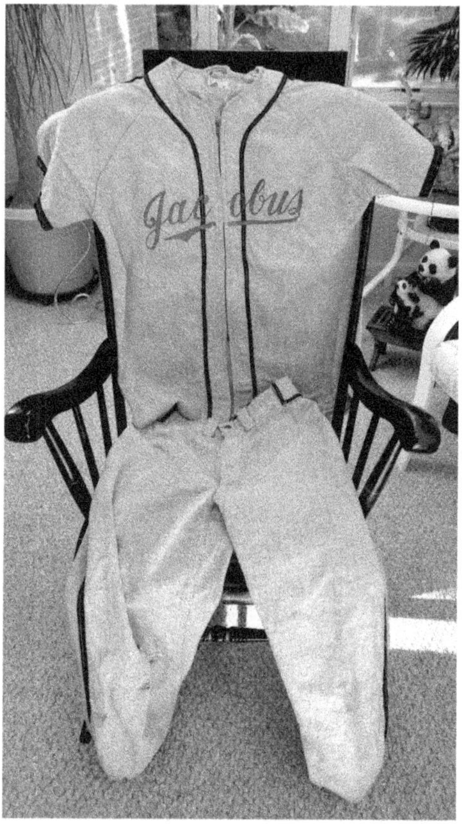

A still-surviving Jacobus Baseball uniform from the 1950's – light gray with red lettering and red and black trim. (Uniform provided by Gene Snyder)

A still-surviving Jacobus Baseball uniform from the 1950's – light gray with red lettering and red and black trim. (Uniform provided by Gene Snyder)

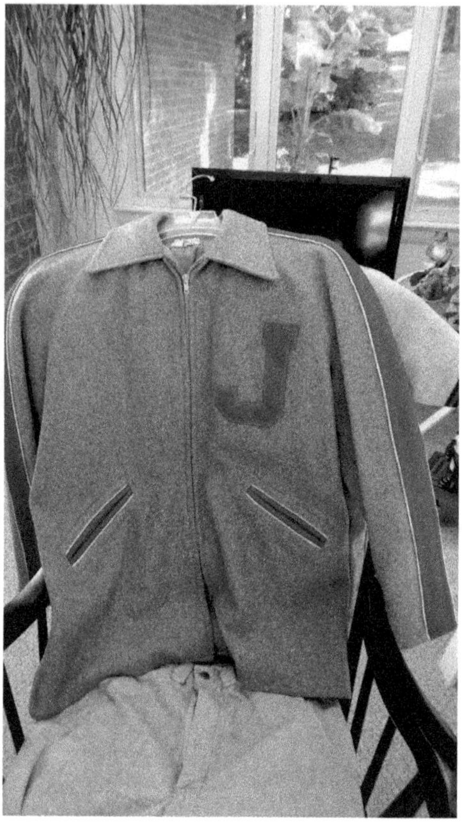

A warm-up jacket from around the same. (Jacket provided by Gene Snyder).

Something new for 1950! The first fund raising carnival is being held for four nights in August 1950 on the grounds behind the Jacobus Fire Hall. The new Fire Hall has just been built and is on the corner of Main Street (Route 111) and York Road. Wandering around on the tar tab parking lot behind the new Fire Hall, one of the big attractions for everyone is the Ferris Wheel. The Ferris Wheel is located in the far corner of the parking lot, when facing things from York Road. For a little kid especially, this is a magical event filled with lights, rides, smells, noise, and lots of people. The view from the top of the Ferris Wheel is spectacular as you could look out over the south end of town. Although little kids are not allowed to participate in some of the games of chance, the big wheel is one of my favorites to watch. A lot of folks are plopping down a lot of money to win prizes; everything from candy to cigarettes. There is a ring toss game that even the kids are allowed to participate in, where you can try your luck getting a ring to land over the top of a soda bottle. You can take your pick of a prize if you lucked out. With Mom and Dad's permission the kids are also allowed to participate in the penny and nickel pitch, where you throw your hard-earned candy money on a flat board with numbered squares. They spin the wheel and if your coin is on a selected square, you win a prize. Whether or not you win anything, the carnival gets to keep your penny or nickel! Another of the big attractions is the food, and nothing is better than French fries with salt and vinegar at a carnival. Another big hit is the ice cream waffle – two waffles with a slab of strawberry, chocolate, and vanilla ice cream mix in between.

In 1950, the Jacobus second team is once again Champions of the City County League. As a side note, in the team photo on the following page, Steve Hershner is shown as the bat boy. Seven years later this Jacobus native will be playing with Buffalo, a Philadelphia Phillies minor league team. He played minor league ball from 1957 to 1961. My uncle Lee filled in some details about Steve Hershner – "In 1955 we had a young player (Steve) about four years younger than me who was also a catcher with good size and ability. His father (Pret Hershner) was our manager, so he came to me and asked if I would be willing to play another position so Steve could catch. He thought that he may have the chance to play professional ball. I asked where I would play, and he asked where I wanted to play, and I said center field. So, he said okay. When Steve graduated he was signed by the Phillies for $4000 – the maximum amount you could sign for at that time – or you had to be put on the Major League roster. He played three years advancing each year in the Phillies system but was always getting hurt."

1950 City County League Champs. Down front: Steve Hershner – bat boy, Front row: Carl Red Arnold, Gene Snyder, Bob Arnold, Vernon Geiselman, Larry Smith, Amos Warfel, Gerald (Bob) Schrum. Back row: Pret Hershner – manager, Charlie Smith, Clarke Jake Shearer, Richard Bupp, Earl Easter Hildebrand, Marvin Lee Arnold, Dale Innerest, Perry Innerst, Jr. (Photo taken in Felton, PA. courtesy of Carl "Red" Arnold)

Photo taken in same location in Felton, PA. as the previous one, but in 2017. (Note the old home still standing in the background. Although not visible in this photo because of the new buildings in the foreground, the barn on the far right in the original photo is also still standing - but barely.)

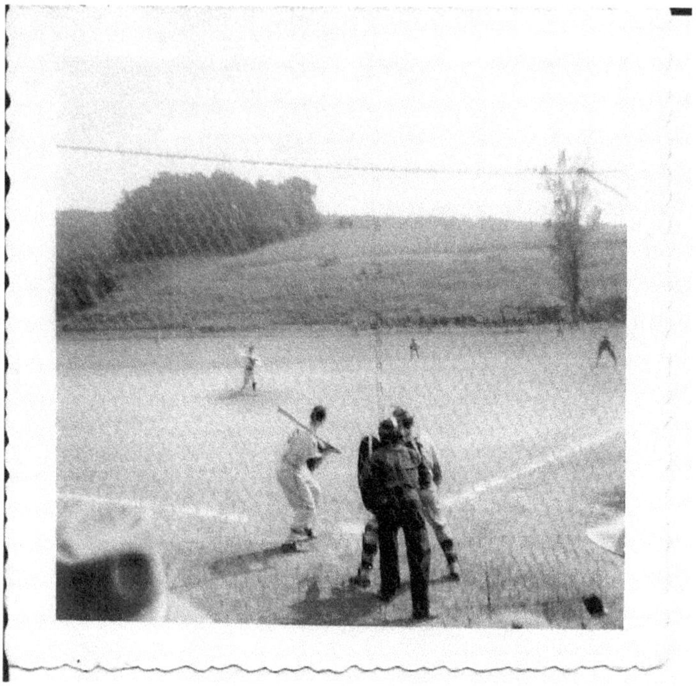

1950 in Felton, PA. (Photo courtesy of Carl "Red" Arnold)

1951 – After the Major League Baseball season was over, a lot of the players formed "barnstorming" teams and would go from city to city and play area All-Star Teams to make additional money. At that time the professional players needed off season jobs to support themselves because of their low salaries. In 1951 one of these All-Star games was held locally at York's Memorial Stadium. Here's something from my uncle Lee's recollections of one of those games – "I was called by Dutch Dorman, a local Phillies Scout, and he said that he needed another catcher for the All-Star game. He asked if I wanted to play. Naturally, I said yes, as most of the players were Minor League or Ex Minor League players. Uncle Sterling Arnold was one of the pitchers, as he was pitching for Red Lion at the time. I caught three innings while he pitched and had one at bat against Frank Smith, who pitched for Cincinnati at the time. I popped up to the first baseman. I was only 16 years old and this was the highlight of my life… playing against big leaguers… primarily from the Reds and the Phillies. Some of the players in the game were Del Enis, Robin Roberts, Connie Ryan, Sibby Sisty, and Andy Semenich."

(Author's note – Frederick "Dutch" Dorman was a long-time minor league baseball player and manager who later scouted for the Philadelphia Phillies and Atlanta Braves.)

—Photo by The Gazette and Daily

FURNISHED OPPOSITION FOR MAJOR LEAGUERS—The York County All-Stars, above, competed against the touring Major League All-Stars in the game played yesterday at Memorial Stadium as a benefit for the stadium building fund.

The players from York County included: Front row, left to right, Ned Kopp, Billy Koyalak, Gene Snyder, Glenn Leiphart, Lee Arnold, Leon Senft, Don Smith, Bill Moul and manager Fred (Dutch) Dorman; back row, coach Ralph (Abe) Simpson, Dean Royer, Bill Plate, Charles Witmer, Marlyn Holtzapple, Heckert Horn, Sterling Arnold, Sam Miller, Wayne Heim, Ray Shearer and Bill Riale. Bat boy Jack Fasick is shown in the foreground.

The Major Leaguers won the game, 7 to 1.

The 1951 York County All Star Team (Uncle Lee is sitting right behind the bat boy. Lee's uncle Sterling Arnold is 5th in from the right in the back row.) (Courtesy of York Heritage Trust Library/Archives)

All Stars Article, next page (Courtesy of York Heritage Trust Library/Archives)

OCT 9 1951
22 The Gazette and Daily, York, P

List Local Stars Scheduled To Play In Benefit Game Sunday At Stadium

Gene Snyder, Ray Shearer, Wayne Heim and Marlyn Holtzapple on county squad to oppose Major leaguers. Raffensberger to hurl for major stars in game starting at 2 p. m. Proceeds go to Memorial stadium.

A quartet of promising York County baseball players who performed very well in organized baseball during the past season, several present and former members of the York White Roses and a group of outstanding county league standouts will compose the York County-All-Stars aggregation for its battle here Sunday with the touring Major League All-Stars.

The game, for the benefit of the Memorial Stadium corporation, will be played at the stadium starting at 2 p.m.

Gene Snyder, Ray Shearer, Marlyn Holtzapple and Wayne Heim are the four youthful stars who have recently returned home after successful seasons in various sections of the country.

Snyder, a former Pleasureville pitching star, just completed a splendid season with Salina, Kan., in the Class C Western Association.

The youthful speedball artist, who is the property of the Philadelphia Phillies, won 17 and lost ten during the season and hung up the excellent record of 230 strikeouts.

Shearer finished the recent season with Ashville, N. C., in the Class B Tri-State league. The former Jacobus player compiled a .285 batting average as an outfielder and is scheduled to jump to Pueblo, Colo., in the Class A Western league next season. He is in the Brooklyn Dodger system.

Marlyn Holtzapple, former Stoverstown product, is the property of the St. Louis Browns who recently signed a working agreement with the York White Roses. Holtzapple was with Pine Bluff, Ark., in the Cotton States league during the past season and is one of the most highly regarded younger shortstops in the Browns' system.

Wayne Heim, who formerly played for East Prospect, compiled a batting average in excess of .300 while playing the outfield in the Wisconsin State league during the past season.

Two members of the 1951 White Roses, Bruce Smith, a third baseman, and Bill Plate, an outfielder, are expected to play.

Billy Kovalak, most valuable player of the Southern York County league, and a former member of the York White Roses is also on the York County roster.

Other outstanding county players are: Lee Arnold, Jacobus; Bill Soul, Jefferson; Dean Royer and Eckert Horn, Red Lion, and Don Smith, Hallam. The latter turned down several major league offers during the past year and had a spectacular record with the Hallam nine of the Twilight league.

Several other players are yet to be contacted by Fred (Dutch) Dorman, who will manage the York County team against the Major leaguers. Dorman's Hagerstown club won the pennant in the Interstate league during the 1951 season.

Ralph "Abe" Simpson, who has helped develop several outstanding young players during the past several years with the Yankee A. A. Junior Legion teams will help coach the county nine.

Raffensberger To Pitch

York's own Ken Raffensberger is expected to pitch part of the game for the touring Major leaguers.

Other members of Danny Litwhiler's All-Stars are: Ray Mueller, Carl Furillo, Montia Kennedy, Sibby Sisti, Bill Howerton, Bill Nicholson, Nelson Fox, Frank Smith, Carl Scheib and Danny Murtaugh. The latter was recently named manager of the New Orleans nine.

Tickets On Sale

Reservations for tickets can be made by calling Memorial Stadium corporation 87246 or contacting Ashmer C. Owen in the city treasurer's office at City hall.

An official of the stadium announced last night that the York Bus company will run special buses to the stadium for Sunday's game.

Another player from Jacobus, Ray Shearer, was mentioned in this article about the local All-Star game, and in the team picture is 2nd in from the right in the last row. Ray Shearer, Jr., also known as "Junie" signed with the Brooklyn Dodgers minor league organization in 1950. He was traded to the Milwaukee Braves minor league organization in 1956. He played two Major League games for the Braves in 1957. His professional baseball career ended in 1962.

Here's more background about the leagues from my uncle Lee – "The summer of 1951 I played for the Jacobus first team, in the Southern League. Stewartstown had Dick Hall, who later pitched for the Orioles. The caliber of players in the leagues was very good. There were former professional players on many teams. In the early fifties, most teams paid at least one or two players $10 to $20 a game and some fans would give some money to someone that hit a home run to win a game. At one time, there were seven Arnolds on the second team."

Just in case you were wondering, baseball and basketball weren't the only sports that were played locally. Although not quite as popular as baseball back then, football made a short appearance in Jacobus around this time. Here's more from uncle Lee - "When I was sixteen we also had a town football team that played Sunday afternoons. This was mostly older boys that played. We had a few players that played in High School. The ages were from about 16 to 21. We had a guy that didn't play that coached. We would have practice and on Friday nights we would go as a team to Smith's Store and sit on the floor in front of a TV and watch College Football Highlights to learn plays and skills of the game. We used the single wing formation with Red Arnold (Author - my Dad) calling the signals. Rich Arnold (Author - my uncle) and I played in the backfield. Bob Arnold (Author - my uncle) played in the line. We had some big guys on the line .... Mostly older players.... And they were good blockers and I was fast and could make good yardage. We had some of the Snyders, John Lacondro, Perry Innerst, and Paul Innerst playing also. We were playing in East York one time and Russ Shearer was there watching the game and... I don't know if somebody got hurt... and he said 'Well, I'll play'. So, he came in and ended up breaking his collarbone." Uncle Bob mentioned, "Doc Getz would come out to our football games on Sunday afternoon in case someone got hurt.". Uncle Lee continues – "We played our games out on the baseball diamond, from the right field foul line down to the road. We usually did well except for some of the teams we played from York. One time we played a team from Dallastown after their High School schedule was over and they thought they would cream us because they won the County League and had players that were out of school too. We beat them in a rough fought game. We only had helmets and shoulder pads and some of the older players that had jobs bought football shoes. The rest wore sneakers or clod hoppers. We put on a play and had bake sales to raise money to pay for helmets and shoulder pads and we did buy good helmets. I got knocked out one time. When I came to, I was sitting in a car watching the game and looked to my feet and I had football shoes on, but I didn't own any. I asked where I got the shoes and was told Rich (Arnold) got hurt and I put his shoes on at half time and got tackled hard and had to be taken out of the game also. They said I was on the side lines telling them to put me back in the game, but I didn't remember that. I told my brothers not to tell Mom or she would not let me play. I believe that football lasted just a few years and the interest dwindled and we disbanded." What my uncle Bob had to say may have been a good reason that football didn't last too long in town. He was laughing when he said – "We'd be all beat up on Monday or Tuesday and Mom would get tired of it… she said, 'If you want to kill yourself, go kill yourself! What do I care…' (or something like that). As a matter of fact, Monday at work you'd have trouble walking… you couldn't even tie your shoes, we would be so beat up!"

The Baseball for Boys 13 – 15 team took the 1951 championship vs. Shiloh. (Refer to Appendix D. for a photo of the trophy.)

At this point, the basketball team was having some success, to the point that they started being supported by the Athletic Association for things like hall rentals, etc. They were winning at least 50% of their games and continuing to improve.

1952 – The pattern had pretty well been set at this point for continuing the business of the Athletic Association - purchasing supplies, uniforms, and maintaining the field as needed.

The Baseball for Boys (13 – 15) team received a championship runner-up trophy this year. (Refer to Appendix D. for a photo of the trophy.)

Things became more interesting toward the end of the year when discussions started regarding building some kind of a permanent concession stand and storage area at the ball diamond.

An even more important thing happened when the Athletic Association approved a motion to begin the purchase of another large piece of land from Mont Smith, described as “the land opposite the ball field”. This is the property across Pleasant Avenue from the ball diamond where the basketball court, tennis court, and other facilities are now located.

1953 – Some big field improvement projects took place during this year. A cement block storage and concession stand building was constructed behind the home plate backstop. A water line was run up to the ball diamond from a nearby water main. Again, a number of people chipped in to make this happen with their skills and labor, including Clair Smith, Pete Shearer, Jake Meyers, Jesse Keeney, and Ralph Innerst.

Money was put down on the purchase of the additional property across Pleasant Avenue. At this point in time, no one was really sure yet what would be done with this new property.

The Baseball for Boys team was once again 1953 champs. They were treated to a banquet by the Athletic Association to celebrate. (See the photos of the trophy in Appendix D.)

1954 – This was a year when attention was put on bringing in new members and putting work into the newly purchased property. The new property is now being referred to as the “playground” in the Athletic Association minutes. It was plowed, leveled, and planted with grass seed.

There was also the possibility of moving a storage shed into center field behind the flag pole.

For a short period, this year, the Athletic Association owned a 1935 Chevy as a utility vehicle. It appears though that trying to drag a mower with it only tore apart the mower! The Chevy didn’t stick around long and was sold. A motion was made to start looking for a tractor instead.

Once again, the Baseball for Boys team was involved in the league playoffs and ended up 1954 runner-up’s. (See the photos of the trophy in Appendix D.)

1955 – With another year beginning, things were continuing to move along with the routine established in past years. The Carnival committee was appointed for the year, continuing that fund-raising activity.

The Baseball for Boys program was expanding into a newly formed Southern League.

Swings were added to the new playground area.

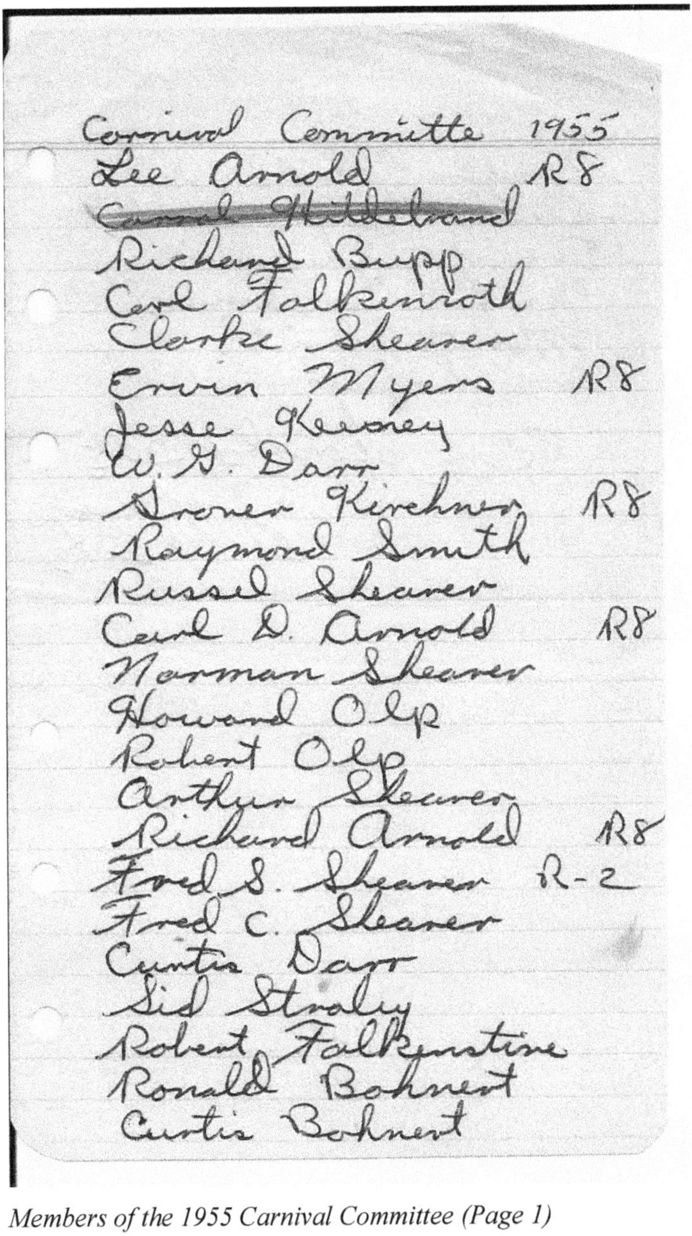

Carnival Committe 1955
Lee Arnold R8
~~Carrol Hildebrand~~
Richard Bupp
Carl Falkenroth
Clarke Shearer
Ervin Myers R8
Jesse Kearney
W. G. Darr
Grover Kirchner R8
Raymond Smith
Russel Shearer
Carl D. Arnold R8
Norman Shearer
Howard Olp
Robert Olp
Arthur Shearer
Richard Arnold R8
Fred S. Shearer R-2
Fred C. Shearer
Curtis Darr
Sid Straley
Robert Falkenstine
Ronald Bohnert
Curtis Bohnert

Members of the 1955 Carnival Committee (Page 1)

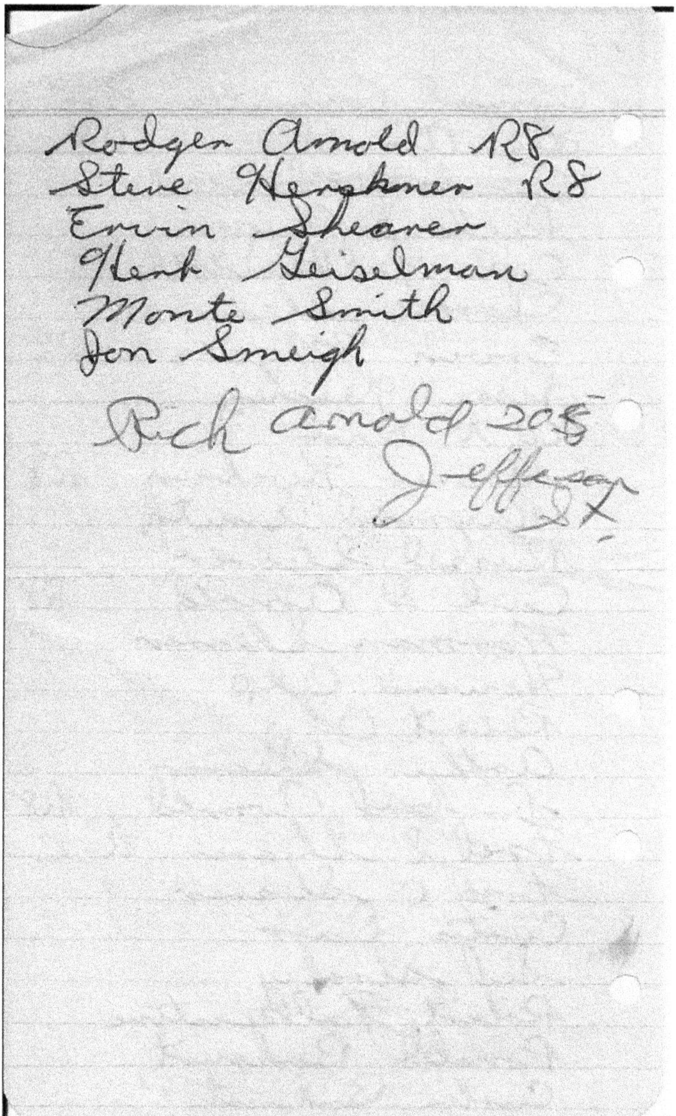
Rodger Arnold R8
Steve Hershner R8
Ervin Shearer
Henk Geiselman
Monte Smith
Jon Smeigh
Rich Arnold 20$
Jefferson Jr.

Members of the 1955 Carnival Committee (Page 2)

...ations in which baseball is now ...ayed, relative to participation.

Baseball-For-Boys Group Is Planned In Southern Area

Jacobus — Representatives of 14 teams attended a meeting here last night for the purpose of forming a Baseball-for-Boys league among teams of the southern York county area.

The group proposes to set up its own organization, for both 8-to-12 and 13-to-15 age divisions. Carroll Hildebrand of Jacobus acted as chairman at last night's session. A nominating committee consisting of Dick Culbertson, Earl Hildebrand and Bill Goodling was directetd to report at the groups' next meeting April 19 at 8 p.m. at the Innerst Trucking company, Jacobus.

Teams which were represented at last night's session were: Jacobus, Winterstown, Glen Rock, Stewartstown, Spry, Dallastown, New Freedom, Loganville, Hallam, Spring Grove, Shrewsbury, Fawn Grove, Conrads and Seven Valleys.

Any county teams interested in the proposed setup are invited to attend the April 19 meeting. A schedule will be considered at the meeting.

APR 7 1955

A Southern Area Baseball for Boys League was being formed in 1955. (Article Courtesy of York Heritage Trust Library/Archives)

1956 – Improvements to the property continue with this year. The access road had some work done to it.

The Athletic Association began looking for a summer playground director this year, although the search was not completely successful. The foundation was being laid however for the excellent future summer programs for kids, which this author took part in (as a kid).

Toward the end of the year, the original dugouts and backstop from 1948 were rebuilt.

The Baseball for Boys league continued to grow and prosper. Sterling Arnold, mentioned earlier was re-elected President of the league.

Arnold Re-Elect Of County BFB League

Jacobus—Sterling Arnold, former minor league baseball player, was re-elected president of the York County Baseball-For-Boys league during a meeting in Innerst's garage here last night.

Other officers named are: Carrol Hildebrand, first vice-president; William Goodling, second vice-president and Sterling Ecker, secretary-treasurer.

Teams from ten towns were represented at the meeting and the final makeup will be made May 7 during another meeting here at 7:30 p.m. Towns wishing to enter teams in either the 8-12 or 13-15 age groups are requested to send representatives.

Attending last night's meeting were: Hallam, Seven Valleys, Jacobus, Red Lion, Stewartstown, Yoe, Glen Rock, New Freedom, Dallastown and Spry.

APR 24 1956

Sterling Arnold re-elected as president of the Baseball for Boys League… (Article Courtesy of York Heritage Trust Library/Archives)

Some things are always in motion… including the ground rules…

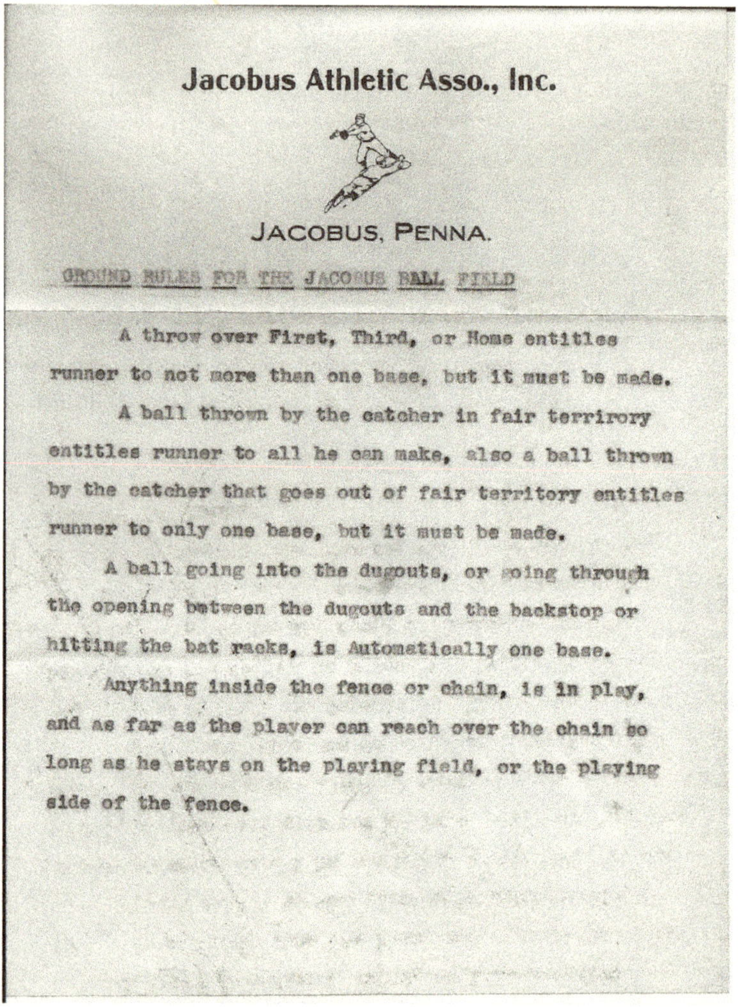

Jacobus Athletic Asso., Inc.

JACOBUS, PENNA.

GROUND RULES FOR THE JACOBUS BALL FIELD

A throw over First, Third, or Home entitles runner to not more than one base, but it must be made.

A ball thrown by the catcher in fair terrirory entitles runner to all he can make, also a ball thrown by the catcher that goes out of fair territory entitles runner to only one base, but it must be made.

A ball going into the dugouts, or going through the opening between the dugouts and the backstop or hitting the bat racks, is Automatically one base.

Anything inside the fence or chain, is in play, and as far as the player can reach over the chain so long as he stays on the playing field, or the playing side of the fence.

An update to the ground rules made in 1956…

1957 – The Carnival event happened again this year, in addition to the yearly work on the ball diamond. Judging by the lack of Association minutes, this was a quiet year.

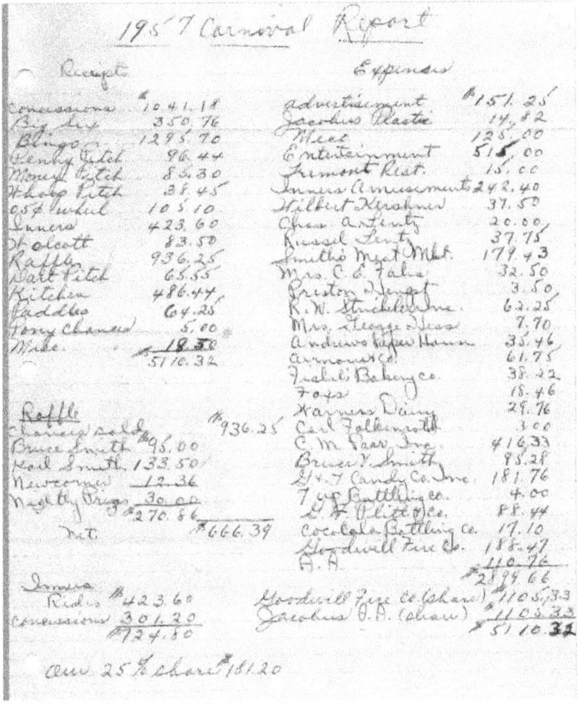

1957 Carnival Report

Receipts		Expenses	
Concessions	$1041.18	Advertisement	$151.25
Big Six	350.76	Jacobus Plastic	14.82
Bingo	1295.70	Meat	125.00
Penny Pitch	96.44	Entertainment	515.00
Money Pitch	85.30	Fremont Rest.	15.00
Hoop Pitch	38.45	Inners Amusements	242.40
05¢ wheel	105.10	Hilbert Kershner	37.50
Inners	423.60	Chas. Lenty	20.00
Holcott	83.50	Russel Lenty	37.75
Raffle	936.25	Smith's Meat Mkt.	179.43
Dart Pitch	65.55	Mrs. C. E. Fahs	32.50
Kitchen	486.44	Preston [illegible]	3.50
Paddles	64.25	R. W. Strickler Inc.	62.25
Pony Chances	5.00	Mrs. George [illegible]	7.70
Misc.	18.30	Andrews Paper House	35.46
	5110.32	Armour Co.	61.75
		[illegible] Bakery Co.	38.22
		Foxs	18.46
		Warners Dairy	29.76
		Carl Folkenroth	3.00
		C. M. Paar, Inc.	416.33
		Bruce V. Smith	95.28
		G & F Candy Co. Inc.	181.76
		7 up Bottling Co.	4.00
		G. F. Plitt Co.	88.44
		Coca Cola Bottling Co.	17.10
		Goodwill Fire Co.	188.47
		A. A.	110.76
			$2899.66
		Goodwill Fire Co. (share)	$1105.33
		Jacobus O. A. (share)	$1105.33
			$5110.32

Raffle

Chances sold		$936.25
Bruce Smith	$95.00	
Neil Smith	133.50	
Newcomer	12.36	
Naughty Bugs	30.00	
	$270.86	
Net		$666.39

Inners

Rides	$423.60
Concessions	301.20
	$724.80

Our 25% share $181.20

Carnival receipts and expenses from 1957...

York County 8- BFB All-Star Squad Named

Coach Lowell Henry and his assistants, Lee Arnold and Gene Snyder, yesterday announced the personnel of the York County 8-12 All Star team which will meet the Susquehanna BFB club in a three-game series next week. Winner will earn the right to represent York County in th Mason-Dixon tournament.

The first game in the series will be played Monday at Manchester at 6 p.m. with the second slated for Wednesday at 6 p.m. on the Jacobus diamond. Arrangements for a third game, if needed, will be made later.

JUL 27 1957

Henry announced that the York County team would practice tomorrow at 1:30 p.m. on the Jacobus field and all players are to report promptly.

Members of the squad and their teams are: Red Lion, Larry Orwig, Charles Horn and Barry Strayer; Fawn Grove, Leslie Pomraning; Seven Valleys, Glen Smith, Stuart Markle, and Jack Harrold; Wrightsville, Michael Hinds and James Townsley; Hallam, Freddie Dellinger and Donald Meyers; Yoe, Sidney Culbertson and Wayne Sawicki; Glen Rock, Donald Schnell and Terry Yohe; Stewartstown, John Johnson and Paul Godfrey; Jacobus, Mark Innerst and Robert Stremmel; Brogue, Robert Workinger and Rodger Holtzinger; New Freedom, Toby Masenheimer; Dallastown, Barry Attig and Ernest Smeltzer.

1957 Baseball for Boys 8 – 12 league All Stars. Players from Jacobus – Robert Stremmel and Mark Innerst. Mark Innerst would later go on to be a Jacobus summer Playground Director... (Article Courtesy of York Heritage Trust Library/Archives)

1958 – Things were mostly quiet this year on the Athletic Association front however, both the first and second baseball teams did well. The second team won the Amateur League Championship and the first team was runner-up in the Central League.

Amateur League Champs – George Arnold, Paul Arnold, Roger Arnold, Ted Arnold, William Arnold, Barry Shearer, Gene Shearer, Dane Shearer, Merv Slenker (Mgr.), Whitey Kershner (coach), Jerry Darr, Pete Klein, Frank Curry, M. Dise, Don Smith, Barry Shearer, Jack Shearer, Dale Warfle, Don Arnold (Scorer), Don Slenker (Scorer).

Central League Runner-ups – D. Innerst (Dale), N. Shearer (Norman (Bud)), R. Shearer (Russell), L. Williams (Les), G. Snyder (Gerry)?, C. Folkenroth (Carl), R. Riese (Ronald), M. Keeney (Jess (Min)), D. Kerns (Donald (Duck)), J. Snyder (Jay), R. Arnold (Richard), R. Bohnert (Ronald), A. Shearer (Arthur (Pete)), B. Shearer (Barry), Gene Snyder, L. Arnold (Lee), D. Stagemyer (Donald). (See Appendix D. for photos of the trophies.)

This was also the first year that the Donkey Baseball fund-raiser was held. See the chapter called "The Money Game" for a description of Donkey Ball.

1959 – This is a year of change. As I mentioned in the Introduction - interests change and life starts to get in the way. The original founders of the Athletic Association are now all knee deep in raising and supporting their families. Things in the Athletic Association had stabilized and are mostly in "maintenance mode".

Motions are being made and discussions are being held about turning over the ball field and playground property to the Jacobus Borough and then chipping in to pay for use of the property. As mentioned in Appendix A., on **June 30, 1959** the property officially passed from the Jacobus Athletic association to the Jacobus Borough for $1. As mentioned elsewhere in this book, part of the reason for this was to guarantee the property would always remain as a ballfield and playground.

During this year the position of "playground director" became more established. This eventually becomes a position that instructs, supervises, and manages the summer baseball and playground programs.

The Money Game

Baseball is too much of a sport to be called a business and too much of a business to be called a sport.

— Cubs owner Phil Wrigley

Through the years…

From the very beginning, even before the Jacobus Athletic Association was formed, the town baseball teams had various fund-raising projects going on all the time. As mentioned in previous chapters, it was necessary to pay the umpires, buy baseballs and uniforms, and all of that kind of thing. In addition, there were some local businessmen, over the years, who went above and beyond to provide support and funds when the needs came up. From the beginning of the Athletic Association, local men like Sam Babble and Nevin Smith provided much needed funds. Later on, the Smith's from the Smith Village store complex were great contributors of time and money. These individuals were far from the only means of support however. In general, the entire community always seemed to support and provide for the needs of the baseball program and the Athletic Association.

It took a lot of work to support a team. It would be hard to count the number of hours of volunteer labor, time, and expertise contributed over the years. The key word here is "contributed". No salaries were being paid to anyone for any of these labors, yet things still got done. To quote my Dad once again, "I don't remember we ever had a problem in buying anything, because there were people that were willing to donate money to keep the team going."

The "hat" was always passed among the spectators at the games for anyone who wanted make a donation. As a little kid I remember throwing in a nickel or so of my candy money every once in a while, or talking my mom or dad or an uncle into giving me some money so I could contribute.

One money making project for many years was the "Scorecard". This was a 14 by 11-inch light weight cardboard sheet. In the center of the scorecard was the standard baseball grid for "keeping score" of players runs, hits, and errors, etc. Filling the back of the card and surrounding the scoring area on the front side, were blocks which local businesses could purchase for advertising space. The message on the back from the Jacobus

Athletic Association was "Please Patronize Our Advertisers". The ads went for $5.00 or more a block. If you had a large block it cost you more than the smaller block ads. Almost <u>every</u> business in the area supported the Association by buying one or more blocks.

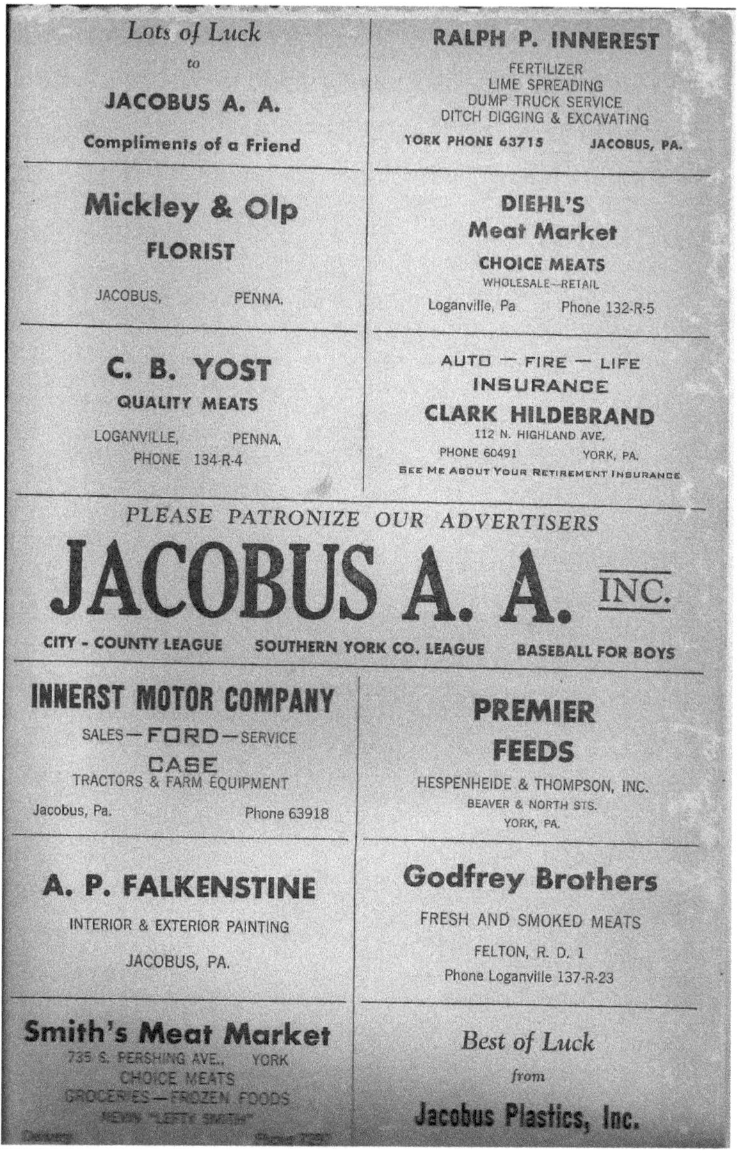

Lots of Luck
to
JACOBUS A. A.
Compliments of a Friend

RALPH P. INNEREST
FERTILIZER
LIME SPREADING
DUMP TRUCK SERVICE
DITCH DIGGING & EXCAVATING
YORK PHONE 63715 JACOBUS, PA.

Mickley & Olp
FLORIST
JACOBUS, PENNA.

DIEHL'S
Meat Market
CHOICE MEATS
WHOLESALE—RETAIL
Loganville, Pa Phone 132-R-5

C. B. YOST
QUALITY MEATS
LOGANVILLE, PENNA.
PHONE 134-R-4

AUTO — FIRE — LIFE
INSURANCE
CLARK HILDEBRAND
112 N. HIGHLAND AVE.
PHONE 60491 YORK, PA.
SEE ME ABOUT YOUR RETIREMENT INSURANCE

PLEASE PATRONIZE OUR ADVERTISERS

JACOBUS A. A. INC.

CITY - COUNTY LEAGUE SOUTHERN YORK CO. LEAGUE BASEBALL FOR BOYS

INNERST MOTOR COMPANY
SALES—FORD—SERVICE
CASE
TRACTORS & FARM EQUIPMENT
Jacobus, Pa. Phone 63918

PREMIER
FEEDS
HESPENHEIDE & THOMPSON, INC.
BEAVER & NORTH STS.
YORK, PA.

A. P. FALKENSTINE
INTERIOR & EXTERIOR PAINTING
JACOBUS, PA.

Godfrey Brothers
FRESH AND SMOKED MEATS
FELTON, R. D. 1
Phone Loganville 137-R-23

Smith's Meat Market
735 S. PERSHING AVE., YORK
CHOICE MEATS
GROCERIES—FROZEN FOODS

Best of Luck
from
Jacobus Plastics, Inc.

Back left half of a scorecard from 1952. Advertising space was sold to support the Jacobus Athletic Association.

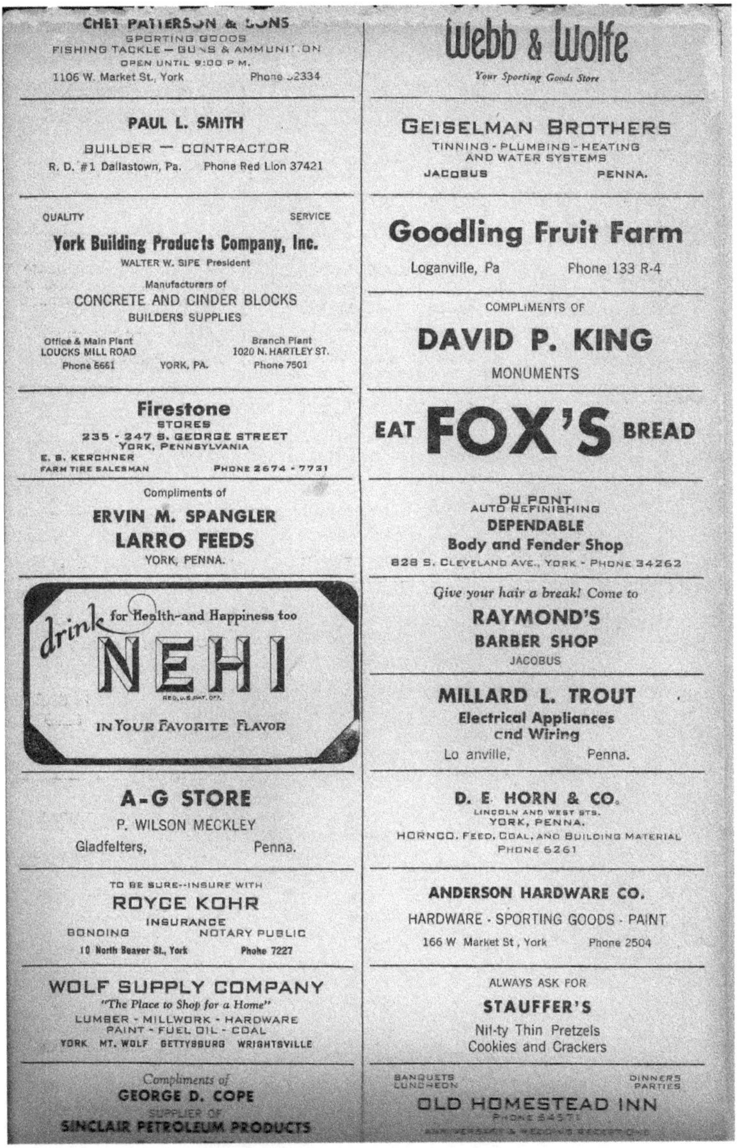

Back right half of a scorecard from 1952. Advertising space was sold to support the Jacobus Athletic Association.

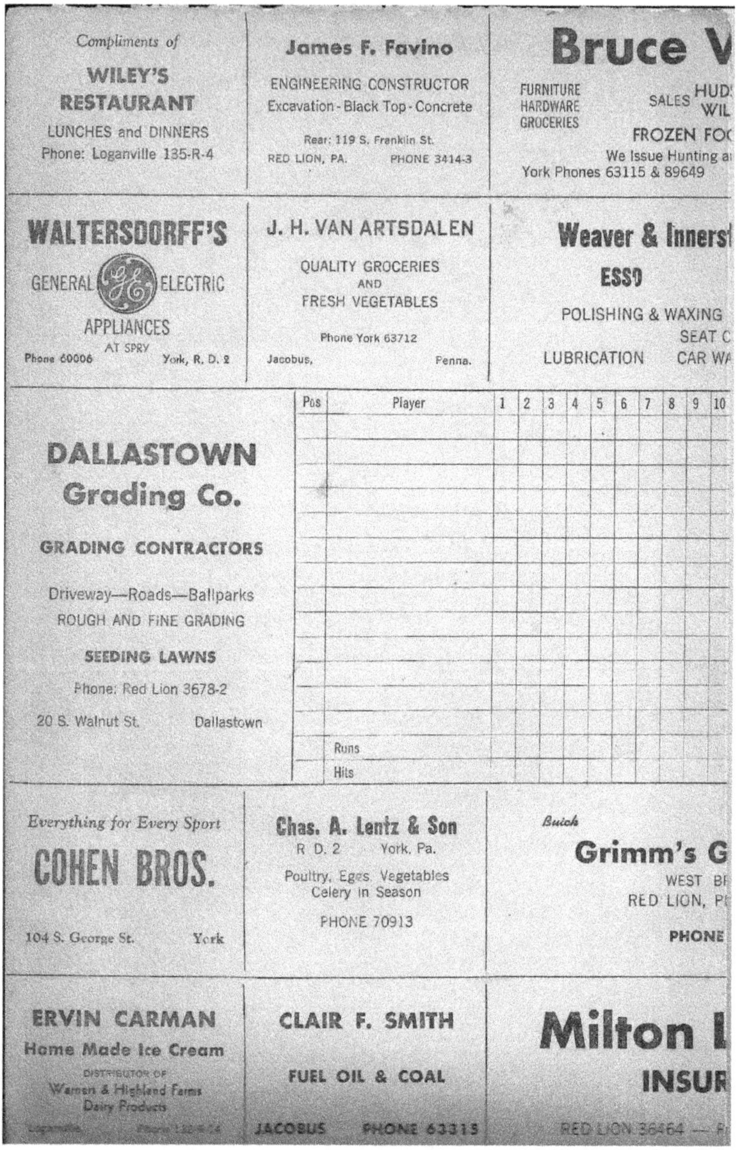

Compliments of
WILEY'S RESTAURANT
LUNCHES and DINNERS
Phone: Loganville 135-R-4

James F. Favino
ENGINEERING CONSTRUCTOR
Excavation - Black Top - Concrete
Rear: 119 S. Franklin St.
RED LION, PA. PHONE 3414-3

Bruce V
FURNITURE
HARDWARE
GROCERIES
SALES HUD
WIL
FROZEN FO
We Issue Hunting a
York Phones 63115 & 89649

WALTERSDORFF'S
GENERAL ELECTRIC
APPLIANCES
AT SPRY
Phone 60006 York, R. D. 2

J. H. VAN ARTSDALEN
QUALITY GROCERIES
AND
FRESH VEGETABLES
Phone York 63712
Jacobus, Penna.

Weaver & Inners
ESSO
POLISHING & WAXING
SEAT C
LUBRICATION CAR WA

DALLASTOWN Grading Co.
GRADING CONTRACTORS
Driveway—Roads—Ballparks
ROUGH AND FINE GRADING
SEEDING LAWNS
Phone: Red Lion 3678-2
20 S. Walnut St. Dallastown

Pos	Player	1	2	3	4	5	6	7	8	9	10
	Runs										
	Hits										

Everything for Every Sport
COHEN BROS.
104 S. George St. York

Chas. A. Lentz & Son
R. D. 2 York, Pa.
Poultry, Eggs, Vegetables
Celery in Season
PHONE 70913

Buick
Grimm's G
WEST B
RED LION, P
PHONE

ERVIN CARMAN
Home Made Ice Cream
DISTRIBUTOR OF
Warren & Highland Farms
Dairy Products

CLAIR F. SMITH
FUEL OIL & COAL
JACOBUS PHONE 63313

Milton I
INSUR
RED LION 36464 — P

Front left half of a scorecard from 1952. Advertising space was sold to support the Jacobus Athletic Association.

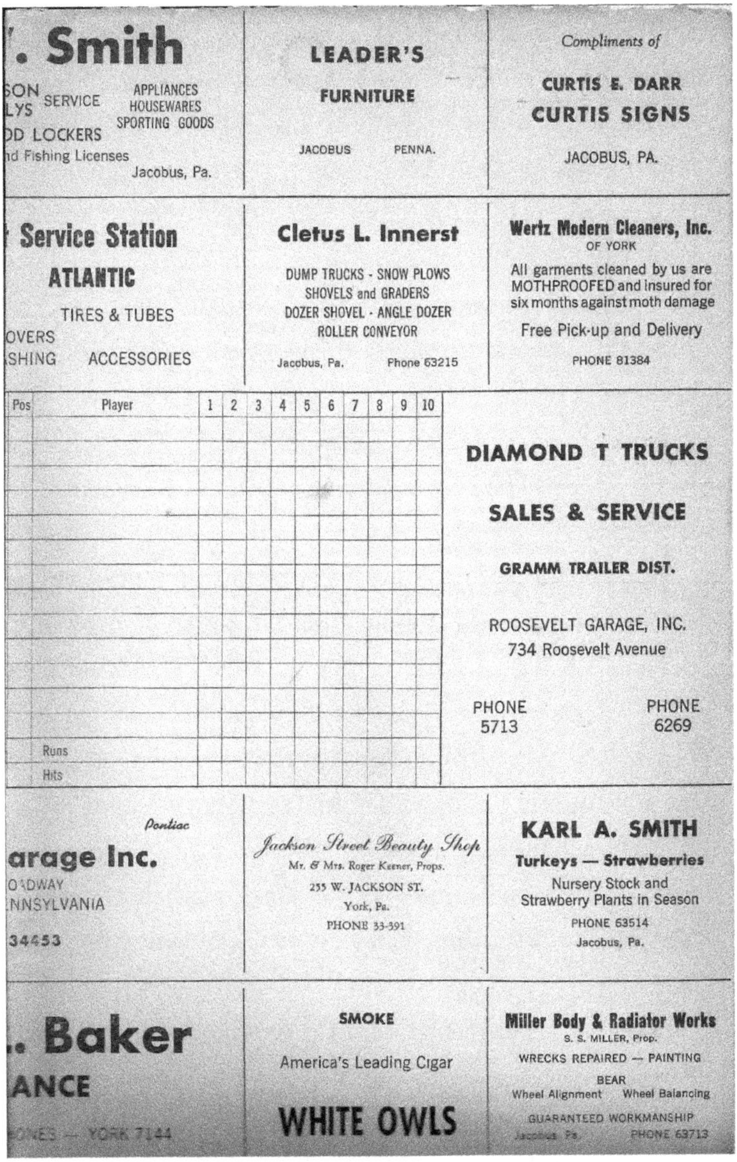

Front right half of a scorecard from 1952. Advertising space was sold to support the Jacobus Athletic Association.

Businesses also purchased advertising space on the score board.

There was always a concession stand at the games, stocked with plenty of soda, candy, gum... just about anything that could be resold for some funds. Big sellers were all the different kinds of soda available at the time (all of the Nehi flavors, RC Cola, Upper 10, etc.), candy bars, and (of course) Cracker Jacks. My grandfather Howard Olp, besides serving on the Association's board of Directors, spent a lot of time selling from the concession stand. Juice (George) Keeney, John Schroll, and Huntz (Allen) Falkenstine also served as concessionaires at the beginning.

Bake sales were another form of raising funds. My uncle Lee sold his "world famous" peanut butter fudge. He mentioned, "I believe I have made over 1000 lbs. of fudge in my time." There were also films shown and picnics held as fund raisers. One of the films shown in 1950 included pictures from the 1949 World Series and a serial on "Snuffy Smith".

Although the author doesn't have much information on what went on at these events, there is some mention of "May Day Festivals". These were eventually replaced by the fund-raising carnivals.

The first fund raising carnival was held for four nights in August 1950. It was held on the grounds behind the Jacobus Fire Hall, which was located then, and still is, on the corner of Main Street (Route 111) and York Road. The carnival was the standard Fireman's carnival with rides and games of chance. I personally remember riding the Ferris Wheel, watching folks play the “Coin pitches”, and the “Wheels of Chance”. There was also Bingo held in the Fire Hall. The profit from that first carnival was reported to be $1,681.00, which was not a bad sum of money back then for four nights of hard work. The following year in 1951 it was decided to split the effort and profits with the Jacobus Fire Company. From the Athletic Association minutes, it appears that Carnivals were held as a fund-raising event up until 1960.

One other fundraiser that was a big hit was Donkey Baseball. Nowadays the animal protection organizations would not be too happy about this one, because of the treatment of the donkeys, but it was big entertainment back then. The players would play with a “whiffle” ball. If the batter would get a hit, he would jump on a donkey to round the bases. The other wrinkle is that the fielders would also be on donkeys. Here’s the story from my uncle Lee - “Donkey baseball games were put on by a company from Ohio. The first year we had it they sent advertising materials and tickets and as the day for the game came, we sold only a few tickets, and I was worried sick that we would lose money on this project. I had food ordered to sell so I went to the park feeling terrible about the possibility of losing money. The company came and we set up for the game and as the people started coming for the game, I realized we would not have enough room for everyone on the bleachers that seated 500 people. We got a truck and went to the fire hall and got folding chairs. They had a rope around behind the infield and then we set up those chairs there for additional seating. WSBA (a local radio station) sent their radio celebrities down to play against the local team. There was a local funny guy, Amos Warful, who participated in the event and was hilarious. So, I went from worrying we would not have many people there to wondering where we would put them. It was so successful we had it again for the next couple of years." My brother recalls that this was brought back again for a year or so in the late 1960's.

A donkey baseball game at Jacobus Community Park, circa. 1958. (Photo courtesy of Carl "Red" Arnold)

High Jinks on the Road

Lady, if I was your husband, I'd drink it.

— Umpire Bill Klem to a female heckler who had said if Klem was her husband she'd place poison in his coffee.

1940s

There are also a few interesting stories about things that happened while playing ball games on the road... Once again, here are some from my uncles Bob and Lee and Ted and my Mom and Dad...

Lincoln Way – One more time! – Uncle Bob: "Well, that was the Greater York County League... They had a catcher... Bud Shearers wife got into a fight with... I think the wife of their catcher. There was a pretty bad blood between the two teams."

Uncle Lee: "That was out in West York where their diamond was. I heard the guys say "One more time!". There were adults that were rocking this car… and then Coke… I think Coke Kohr got hit by a soda bottle – by one of the women sitting there. He was standing up at the top of the bleachers and one of the Lincoln Way women hit him with a soda bottle!"

Uncle Ted: Knaubie… one of the umpires, his last name was Knaub… and he was a little guy… and sometimes these little guys, they think that they need to make up for their size you know… he was always getting in arguments… Norman Shearer used to get so mad at him… I think he just wanted to pick him up and throw him…

My Dad and Mom also remembered, "They were rocking a car, and trying to flip it over in back of the school in West York. They had a lot of really, really bad fans. They really liked to fight."

Lucky – Lucky to get in… Dad: "When we went down to Lucky to play, that was the Second Team, you were *Lucky if you got in and then Lucky if you got out*! Whenever we went down there to play, the borough policeman (Harry Becker) would go along with us to give us kind of a show of protection. Lucky is down below Bridgeville… down below Conrads… down in the hollow, close to Delta. You go down and around and it was a ball diamond down there. There was an apartment unit out in the outfield. There were all kinds of verbal encounters down there."

Uncle Lee and Uncle Bob: There were some wild games down there. They were all somewhat older. That was in the City County League. We were primarily in high school and there were a couple of players playing who were a year or two out of high school.

Uncle Ted: "There was a family down there in Lucky… you know like here in Jacobus you had the Shearers and you had the Arnolds…Robertson's… there were a lot of Robertson's there in Lucky… and they were all good ball players"

Carl "Red" Arnold at bat at Lucky field. Date unknown. A creek ran from left field around home plate and out past right field. (Photo courtesy of Carl Arnold)

Dale Innerst on the mound at Lucky field. Date unknown. Note the building in left field. Uncle Bob says that "the left fielder's back would have been toward the building that was Lee Diehl's store. The store was along the main road. I don't remember if you were able to drive down to the ball field, but I don't believe so." Speculation is that this is the same building in the recent photo shown next. (Photo courtesy of Carl Arnold)

This is a photo, taken in 2017, of the area that used to be Lucky field. The field was back in behind the building. My uncle Bob thinks that the building on the left may be what used to be Lee Diehl's store, and what appears beyond left field in the previous photo from the 1940s.

Guts and Glory – Dad: "One time in Yorkana I got hit on the head." (Dad was a catcher.) "They wouldn't let me go back in and play. A guy hit me right on top of the head. It was Pete Shearer or Bud Shearer… I'm not sure… who said, no you're not going back in there! It was Bud I guess, not Pete… The batter, he just swung and hit me on the head but it was right on the top. He was just swinging at a ball."

Uncle Lee: "I was catching a game and there was a play at the plate and there was a high throw and I leaped up to get the throw… The guy who was running, and he was an older guy, he put his shoulder down and hit me in the midsection and knocked me back. I remember a guy that lived two doors up from us… when we lived at the house up from the Smith's store… he was at the game and he came down and he kind of took care of me… I was knocked out of the game."

Uncle Lee: "And then there was a time that we went to York Haven and there was a fight that happened, and there was one bat that a bunch of guys used on the team, and when the fight was over that bat… we couldn't find the bat, because I guess somebody took it… and that was up at York Haven… some wild times!

The Pig Pen incident – Uncle Ted: "I remember at Wiota… One time I remember, I think it was Perry Innerst, someone hit a fly ball in center field and he had to go into the pig pen in center field - he had to go under the fence to get the ball".

My Dad also mentioned about the Pig Pen incident. He said, "The Pig Pen was in center field and Perry Innerst had to jump into the pen to retrieve a ball one time."

(Author) – After checking with a local historian, Albert Rose, here's a clarification on the town name mentioned above… Wiota was in N. Codorus Township in the area of Pigeon Hill – later known as Spring Grove.

Rock in Right – Dad: That was up at Cly…up along the river. That was the Second Team. There was this big rock…

probably bigger than the one that's up here in the corner at Woodland and Pine Street now. (Author – about 4 ft. by 4 ft.) A big rock that you had to just be careful of because it was in right field. To the best of my knowledge it's still up there. (Author – my brother checked it out and took pictures – see below. Sometime since my Dad played there, someone must have gotten tired of it, and removed the rock. There's no rock there anymore. I don't have any pictures of the famous rock from back at that time.)

The ball field at Cly – no more rock in right field as of 2017 (Photo courtesy of my brother Dave Arnold)

Kaboom!

The team in first place on the Fourth of July will win the pennant.

— Unknown origin

Mid-1960's

One of the biggest fundraisers and legacies to come out of all of this, in addition to the Park itself, is the July 4th /Stay-at-home Celebration. As of the date this is being written, this event is still being held. The event's 50th anniversary was recently celebrated.

Here are my uncle Lee's comments about how this event came about back in 1964 - "At one of the Jacobus Recreation Association meetings, I suggested that we have a Fourth of July Stay-at-home event. I wanted the prices cheap enough so that families can come for hot dogs, hamburgers, and stuff. We did the same thing with the barbequed chicken – that families could afford to come out for that. I said that I also wanted fireworks, but I wanted the fireworks to go off as soon as it gets dark rather than wait until eleven o'clock like other surrounding communities. So, we all agreed on those terms."

As a personal observer of this event as a kid, I remember the women sitting there covering their eyes the first couple of years, while these inexperienced guys from the Recreation Association were out lighting the fireworks!

Back to Uncle Lee's commentary; "The first fireworks display was thirty dollars. We had pipes in the ground and Don Smith would load them and I'd light the fuse with a flare. I remember that I burnt my socks one time.

We first rented the racks for the chicken barbeque and then later Red (the author's Dad) and brother Bob (the author's uncle) made racks where they worked, at Jacobus Plastics.

We also had Sky Divers come in about 7:00 PM. The leader of the Sky Divers was a ball player we knew from Mt. Wolf. We gave them a chicken meal for doing this. On a windy day somebody landed in behind the Leader's Furniture and Funeral Parlor one time, but normally they landed on a target that they had set up out in centerfield."

My brother Dean tells this story. He remembers that "Uncle George (Arnold) was protecting the chicken pit one year because they thought that one of the Sky Divers was going to land in the pit on one windy day. The Sky Divers ended up all over Jacobus that year. One year it rained – or the fireworks got wet for some reason – because most of the fireworks were duds. The gunpowder just blew up and made a tremendous noise."

My uncle Bob (Arnold) mentioned that "I had asked what we were going to do if it rains, because they had no protection there at all. (Author – This was before the pavilion was built.) So, I rented a tent from someplace in York. They came out and set up this tent and it cost fifty dollars. This included the tent and the set up and tear down. People could then sit under the tent to eat their meals."

A tent was eventually purchased, and every year a group of volunteers would bring out the tent, ropes, poles, and all, from the borough building, where it was stored, and set it up. It was probably a miracle that no one ever got hurt setting up and tearing down the tent.

Uncle Lee also mentioned that "The crew that did the chicken each year asked to have a roof put over the pit in case of rain, so they would still be able to cook the chicken. So, a volunteer crew did that."

"Each year, the program got bigger making more chicken dinners and larger fireworks. As we set our fireworks off early, the roads to town were lined on both sides with cars to see both the Sky Divers and the Fireworks. It wasn't long until we were known for the best program around. This convinced some of the area towns to start their fireworks early also."

Stands were set up behind the first base line dugout to sell soda, hamburgers, and hot dogs.

In the 60's there were fire truck rides and cake walks. Cake walks were accompanied by local entertainment fixture Sam Keeney on the organ.

More things were added in the 70's – karate demonstrations, the Jacobus Area Chorus, the Dallastown Band, and evening music entertainment after the fireworks. Merv and Dane Slenker would set up a PA booth on top of the concession stand behind home plate and MC the event. (The PA system was provided by Stan Kohr.)

Setting up the July 4th Stay-at-Home tent, circa. 1968. (Photo courtesy of Carl "Red" Arnold)

A Sky Diver landing in the outfield at the July 4th Stay-at-Home celebration, circa. 1981. (Photo courtesy of Malinda Arnold – the author's grandmother)

Swinging for the Fences

It ain't braggin' if you can do it.

— Brash pitcher Dizzy Dean

The 1960's and forward…

The 1960's brought a burst of energy and resources supporting additions and improvements to the baseball field and playground. At this point the property had been turned over to the Jacobus borough and a Jacobus Recreation Association had been formed to take over administration of things. The last entry in the minutes of the Jacobus Athletic Association occurred on April 8th, 1962.

Part of the change going on at this time was that around 1962, the "first" and "second" baseball teams were disbanded.

Here's a description of these times from my uncle Lee – "In 1962 we had to get more and more players from out of town and so we decided to disband the team. There was only a small group of players left that were available to get the baseball diamond into shape for each game and to run the fundraisers. Our officers met and we decided to approach the Jacobus Borough Council about donating the property to them and have them form a Recreation Association to run the Baseball for Boys program and to improve the facilities of the playground." Uncle Lee was appointed to the Association at that time and became very involved for a number of years.

The news was not all bad. The program began to change into something even more interesting. A new wave of support began to come from the community and a new wave of energy went into making this a park for everyone – not just ball players.

Before much else had been built on the "playground" property, the kids played on a rough ball diamond there. There were church softball league games played on the main ball field before the men's baseball teams got re-established at a later date.

Shuffle board courts were installed. The contractor, McLaughlin, donated his time. He also supplied the metal forms to pour the curbing for new tennis courts that were being built. The forms would be set the evening before and then volunteers would come out after work the next day. A cement truck would come, and the cement would be poured and leveled off. The next night the forms would be taken off and moved to another section until it was done. To this day, you can see the "signatures" of a few of the many volunteers, still in the concrete on the eastern outer edge of the tennis courts…

One year the tennis courts were flooded with water in the winter, to create an ice skating rink.

Bob Arnold

Denny Franklin, Don Smith, and Jerry Darr

John Geiselman and Jr. King

Lee Arnold and Ron & Jeff Snyder

RSDAY, MARCH 31, 1977.

INVITING WARM WEATHER brings activity to Jacobus' excellent recreational facilities. Tennis enthusiasts Donnie Delp (serving) and Neil Price (York T-shirt) enjoy a rousing match while (left to right) Tom, Mindi and Paula Phillips look on.

Further down the road *– Here's a photo from the 70's showing that use of the tennis courts was not slowing down in popularity. Note the bell bottom jeans – a sure sign of the seventies. (Article from the York Dispatch Newspaper – March 31, 1977.*

A basketball court was also added, right alongside of the tennis courts, along with a tetherball court.

It wouldn't be long before all the efforts of the community started to get noticed throughout the area. In 1966 the community received honors from the Pennsylvania State Chamber of Commerce.

Public Project Provides Playground
This new recreation field in Jacobus was opened this year on the strength of contributions from the borough's citizens. Background shows the growth potential of the community.

"Public Project Provides Playground" *– Although it's difficult to see all the details, here's a photo that appeared in the Harrisburg Patriot news on July 25th, 1964. The caption says, in part "This new recreation field in Jacobus was opened this year on the strength of contributions from the borough's citizens."*

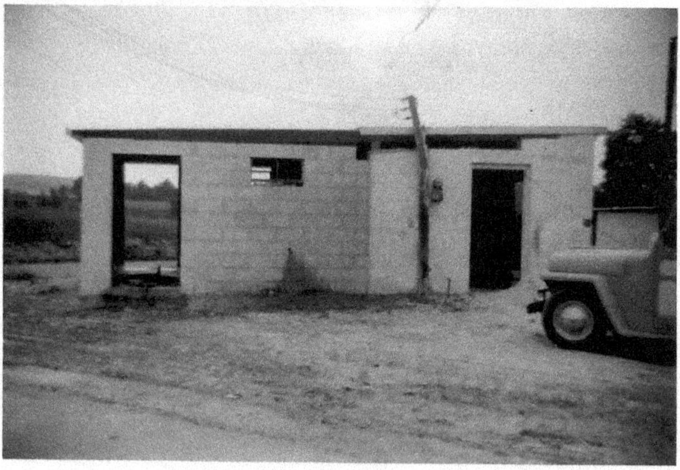

In this photo, construction is in progress on the new restroom facilities, located behind the backstop. It was an addition to the existing storage and concessions stand. - 1964. (Photo courtesy of Carl Arnold)

Thanks to a band of active citizens, the borough of Jacobus has an adequate recreation program and modern facilities.

The work of the Jacobus Recreation Board has won honors from the Pennsylvania State Chamber of Commerce for its "better community development program." The award includes a check for $500, which is to be presented to the board early in July.

Jacobus placed third in Class C competition (for communities with less than 5,000 population) on the basis of its work in directing a workable playground in the community through volunteer efforts of individual residents and business concerns.

Since the board was organized three years ago, it has been responsible for establishing a playground with a basketball court, a shuffleboard court and two tennis courts that can be flooded in winter for ice skating, and supplying play equipment.

A baseball diamond was improved and led to the start of an inter-community boys baseball league.

Officers of the board are: Marvin Arnold, chairman; Mrs. Edward Poff, secretary-treasurer; Mrs. Ronald Bohnert, assistant secretary-treasurer; John Geiselman, member at large; Edwin Shearer and Carl D. Arnold, representing Dallastown Area School Board.

PA Chamber of Commerce Honors *– On June 5th, 1966 a full-page article in the Harrisburg Patriot news discussed the award accompanied by the following photos.*

Jacobus Group Wins Award for Playground

Youths play tetherball *– Mark Innerst, left, playground supervisor at Jacobus, competes with Tom Zartman in a game of tether ball as small boys watch. (Photo courtesy of Harrisburg Patriot News) (Author – my brother Dean is in the striped shirt behind the pole.)*

Inspecting Basketball Court *– Mrs. Carl Folkenroth, left, and Donald Smith board co-chairman, check basketball bank board and net. (Photo courtesy of Harrisburg Patriot News)*

Swings Already in Use *– Susan Folkenroth and Kim Kirchner enjoy the action on the new playground swings. (Photo courtesy of Harrisburg Patriot News)*

Repairing Tennis Courts *– Erwin Shearer, left, and John Geiselman work on wire fence around tennis courts. (Photo courtesy of Harrisburg Patriot News)*

***Everybody Gets in on the Act** – Dallas Smith, left, Ed Keiser, center, and Sam Wildasin, on tractor, help get ball diamond and stands prepared for action. (Photo courtesy of Harrisburg Patriot News)*

Getting Playground in Shape *– Lee Arnold, left, chairman of Jacobus Recreation Association, and Mrs. Edward Poff, board secretary – treasurer, ready grounds for Summer program. (Photo courtesy of Harrisburg Patriot News) (Author – this is my uncle Lee, who's quotes are scattered throughout the book.)*

The author on the mound along with playground directors Owen Statler and Mark Innerst – 1965 (Photo courtesy of Carl Arnold)

As mentioned before, the times were changing and interests were changing also for the original founders of the Jacobus Athletic Association and the Recreation Association. They were becoming custodians of the legacy rather than the ones playing on the field. They tackled the job of custodians just as enthusiastically as they had done when playing on the field, not that many years before.

The 1960's were when some of my friends and I really got to appreciate all that had been done previously, by being able to participate in a summer recreation program that was top notch. That leads us right into the next chapter...

The Big Day

Every time I put the uniform on, I get a thrill.
— Hall of Famer Stan Musial

Summer Mid-1960s

As kids, we loved the game of baseball. My brothers and I had a blast with the other kids in the neighborhood on Pine Street, Jacobus. We were the envy of the other kids in the neighborhood because of our backyard baseball diamond. My Dad had built a kid-sized baseball diamond, backstop and all, in our backyard. Every once in a while, one of the older kids would stop by and we were impressed, because they could bounce hits off of the neighbor's house. The neighbor was not that impressed however, so eventually the older guys were banned. We had a ton of fun on that diamond and learned all we could about the game, while pretending we were Boog

Powell, Davey Johnson, and Brooks Robinson. We thought that we were all pretty good ball players.

Once you were old enough to leave the backyard, you spent your summers, mornings and afternoons every weekday, out at what we called the “Ball Diamond” or the “Playground”. At that time there was an organized summer program going on there, run by the Jacobus Recreation Association. There were playground directors in place there who would serve in whatever capacity they could - as coaches, advisors, baby sitters… whatever. We continued the backyard baseball tradition but now in a bigger neighborhood, with young kids from all over the town, in what were called “town teams”. These were mostly just intramural type teams with kids from the entire community.

Once you were old enough there were also Baseball for Boys teams that you could try out for. There was a league for 8 to 12-year-old kids and another league for the 13 to 15-year-old kids. These teams traveled around to compete with teams from other towns in the area.

As I said, when we were playing in my backyard we thought that we were pretty good. After I left my back yard however, I found out that there were other kids in town that were actually better than us. I loved playing and practicing but the chances were starting to look pretty slim that I would ever see much playing time, other than enjoying the view from the dugout bench. Even if you didn’t have much athletic talent, if you tried out for a team you usually made the team, although as mentioned, you might not see much playing time.

I waited a couple of seasons but then my biggest thrill came when I finally got assigned my own uniform. I don't remember my number, or how long I was allowed to keep it, but I do remember suiting up, jumping on my bike, and riding *slowly* from my house out to the ball park to give all the neighbors a chance to see the new duds. Nothing could be more perfect than being dressed in your baseball uniform and riding your bike out to a game! The uniforms were gray, made of some kind of wool material, and usually pretty hot, but we didn't care. There were socks that had a strap that went over the bottom of your regular socks. Your white socks showed under the strap. You also had rubber or metal spikes to cover the socks. The shirt had the distinctive scripted "Jacobus" lettering on the front in red. The rest of the uniform trim was also red. The caps always had a "J" on the front. Team uniforms, including those for the Jacobus "First" and "Second" teams and the Baseball for Boys Teams were always purchased with money coming from the various fund-raising events that were being held by the Athletic Association and the Jacobus Recreation Association.

My baseball career was not a complete washout. I managed to draw a walk one time from the biggest and most intimidating pitcher in Little League at the time – Jeff Bowman. If I recall, he played for the York Township team. When we found out that he was pitching against us in a game, everyone couldn't help but pay attention – even the best players on our team. Evidently, he was worried that I might actually be able to hit, so he pitched around me… or maybe it was just to set up a force play at third or something… I don't remember that part, but he walked me.

To some of us it felt like this guy was seven feet tall. In another game, I also managed to hit a double over the center fielder's head once when we were playing in Loganville. In that case I think the coach put me in because he was ticked off at all of the first-string players that day. My only regret was that this was a weekday game and that my Dad was not there to see it. He was at work at the time. He would have been impressed to know that I at least had one good hit in my Little League career, and off of a pretty good pitcher at the time, named Dave Hartman.

Celebrating the Good Old Days

Old-timers' weekends and airplane landings are alike. If you can walk away from them, they're successful.

— Manager Casey Stengel

June 1987

Skipping ahead a few decades, in 1987 Jacobus Borough celebrated its 150th (sesquicentennial) anniversary. Part of that celebration included an "old timers" game, played by many of those who helped build the park, and who played ball there over the years. There was a good bit of coverage in the local newspapers. Everyone had a good time playing (no major injuries!) and reminiscing about the "good old days".

Old Timers to help celebrate sesquicentennial

JACOBUS — An "Old Timers" baseball game will be played Saturday as part of the Jacobus Sesquicentennial Celebration.

The game, featuring oldtimers from Jacobus and Loganville, will be played on the Jacobus baseball field at the recreation park along School Road following the Susquehanna League game between Jacobus and York Township, which begins at 1:30 p.m. There will also be musical entertainment following the two baseball games.

The Jacobus "Old Timers," calling themselves the Jacobus City Slickers, have received a challenge from the Loganville "Apple Knockers". The Loganville team is being organized by Congressman Bill Goodling, a native of Loganville who now makes his home in Jacobus.

Several members on the Jacobus Reserve have had professional ball-playing experience. "Heine Heltzel played for the Boston Red Sox, Sterling Arnold with the St. Louis Cardinals and Steve Herschner played Triple A ball with the Phillies organization at Buffalo, New York.

Jacobus "Old Timers" from the 1930's teams will include: "Pallie Innerst, Earl Hildebrand, Erwin Shearer, "Bud" Shearer, "Milt" Diehl, Clair Trout, "Speck" Myers, "Herb" Geiselman, "Chick" Geiselman, "Fritz" Shearer and Carroll Hildebrand.

Players from the 1940's are Paul Smith, Preston Herschner, Perry Innerst, Clark Shearer, Carl Arnold, "Jet" Kenney, Bob Falkenstine, Richard Arnold, C. Richard Bupp, Bill Shearer, Lee Arnold, Roger Arnold, Ted Arnold, Jerre Snyder, Ronnie Snyder, Charles Markey, Walter Ness, Bill Arnold, "Willie" Arnold, Donald Kern, Glen Kline, Sam Jamison, Carl Folkenroth, Dave Eshelman and Clark Hildebrand.

To be qualified to play on the "Old Timers" team a participant should have played on a former Jacobus team and be over 30 years of age and not presently playing organized baseball. Anyone meeting the above qualifications and not already registered to play can do so by contacting any Sesquicentennial Committee member.

Following the ballgames, the Hour Glass Special Edition Band will perform at the recreation park. The group consists of Tina Shaw, rhythm guitar; Jeanne Druck, lead guitar; Mary Ott, bass; and Lonen Reibling, percussionist.

The group plays and sings a variety of music from "Bluegrass to Newgrass", country rock, 50's and 60's classics and just pretty songs in general.

Those attending are asked to bring lawn chairs. The entertainment is being sponsored by Paul Smith Builders.

JACOBUS OLD TIMERS — These former baseball players from Jacobus teams of the 1930's and 40's will play a team of Loganville Old Timers as part of the Jacobus Sesquicentennial Celebration Saturday. From the left, Jacobus Old Timers are: Front — Gene Snyder, Earl Hildebrand and Jess Keeney; Back — Paul Smith, Herby Geiselman, Bud Shearer, Fred Shearer and Clair Trout. The men are holding some of the vintage Jacobus uniforms currently on display at the Sesquicentennial headquarters in the Village Shopping Center, Main Street, Jacobus.

Some of those pictured are names appearing many places throughout this book – First row; Gene Snyder, Earl Hildebrand, Jess Keeney. Second row; Paul Smith, Herb Geiselman, Bud Shearer, Fred Shearer, and Clair Trout. (Article appearing in the York Dispatch Newspaper, June 1987)

Celebration

Old Timers game a part of Jacobus sesquicentennial

By BILL KREIGER
Daily Record correspondent

JACOBUS — An "Old Timers" baseball game Saturday continues the celebration of this community's 150th birthday.

The three-month sesquicentennial celebration was kicked off Memorial Day weekend and included a parade, picnic, entertainment, games and a display of antique cars.

About 4:30 p.m. Saturday, the old timers will take to the community baseball field, located in the southern part of the borough off Main Street, said committee member George Keeney.

"The qualifications require that a player shall have played on a former Jacobus team, must be over 30 years of age and not presently playing on an organized team," Keeney said.

"Jacobus has received challenge from the rival town of Loganville and is preparing to meet the challenge," he said.

The Loganville team is being organized by U.S. Rep. Bill Goodling, R-19, a native of Loganville who now lives in Jacobus.

Goodling said he is looking forward to the game and hopes his team has enough players.

"I've tried to attract their attention," he said noting that his work limited his preparation.

"It'll be different than it used to be, when you had to fight your way out of town after winning the games. It was a tough rivalry then," he said.

"Now we'll be too old to fight our way out of town; that will be the saving grace," he said jovially about those "good old days."

In addition to playing baseball on local teams, Goodling managed baseball for boys and local teams and umpired for the York County League.

He said he enjoyes all aspects of the game, billed as "The Great American Pastime."

The Jacobus roster of players include: Bill "Heine" Heltzel, who played with the Boston Braves; Sterling Arnold, who played in the St. Louis Cardinals system; and Steve Herschner, who was with the Phillies organization (Triple A) at Buffalo.

Among the payers for the local 1930's teams are Earl Hildebrand, Erwin Shearer, Bud Shearer, Milt Diehl, Clair Trout, Speck Myers, Herb Geiselman, Chick Geiselman, Fritz Shearer and Carroll Hildebrand.

Players for the 1940's teams are Paul Smith, Preston Herschner, Perry Innerst, Clark Shearer, Karl Smith, Russel Shearer, Carl Arnold, Jet Keeney, Bob Falkenstine, Richard Arnold, Richard Bupp, Bill Shearer, Lee Arnold, Roger Arnold, Ronald Bohnert, Robert Arnold, Ted Arnold, Earl Arnold, Jerie Snyder, Gene Snyder, Ronnie Snyder, Charles Markey, Walter Ness, Bill Arnold, Willie Arnold, Donald Kern, Glen Kline, Sam Jamison, Carl Folkenroth, Dave Eshelman and Clark Hildebrand.

People meeting the qualifications and wanting to participate in the "Old Timers Game" may contact the celebration committee, Keeney said.

"It has yet to be decided which team — the visiting or home team — will be the 'Taste Great' or 'Less Filling,' " he said.

A concert by the Hour Glass Special Edition will follow the game.

The game and other celebration events are open to the public.

The Jacobus Founding Sesquicentennial headquarters is at 26 Village Shops West, off Main Street and adjacent to Smith Village.

Many old photos and other memorabilia are on display, giving an overview of Jacobus past.

Incorporated in the three-month celebration are the borough's traditional Stay-At Home Fourth of July progr[illegible] and its Labor Day S[illegible]et Fair.

Photo supplied by George Keeney Jr.

Jacobus' first baseball team, as they appeared on Sept. 12, 1908, in Yoe, included, front from left, (no first name available) Arnold and Bill Myers; second row, Harvey Myers, Saul Shearer, Ed Wolf, Ed Darr and Addision Shearer; and third row, Bert Dellinger, (no name avallble), Sal Rohrbaugh, N.J. Leader and Lester Loucks.

Another Sesquicentennial article mentioning the "Old Timers" game. (Article appearing in the York Daily Record Newspaper, June 1987)

1987 - Some of the Old Timers (and not so old timers) game players – Front row; Jake Smith, Rodger Arnold, Rich Arnold, Ron Bonnert, Lee Arnold. Jerry Darr, Jet Keeney, Russ Shearer Back Row; Jake Shearer, Herb Geiselman, Earl Hildebrand, Jeff Trout, Bud Shearer, Ralph Innerst, (no name available), Gene Snyder, Bud Smith, Buck Kern, Dave Eshelman & son. (Photo courtesy of Carl Arnold)

It Ain't Over Yet

It ain't over till it's over.

— Yogi Berra

Spring 2018

As mentioned in the introduction, after the early 1970's I lost track of things going on back home in Jacobus and at the park, since I was living out of the area much of the time. I'm sure a lot has happened since then which adds to the history of the park. From what I have learned recently, the Jacobus Recreation Association has expanded to include more area communities, which still help to support the kids' programs and provide other services. This organization is now called the Jacobus, Loganville, Springfield Township (JLS) Association. The area Lions and Lioness's clubs have helped with events like maintaining the Jacobus 4th of July Celebration tradition, and I'm told that there is currently a men's baseball team called the Jacobus Jackals. I will leave it to someone else to fill in the blanks some day, and to add their stories from the more recent decades to the stories included here.

You are standing with your eyes closed behind home plate in a baseball park in your home town of Jacobus, PA., drifting back to a favorite place in memory from all those years ago. You can still hear the crack of the ball on a bat, the cheering, the yelling, the sounds of the player's chatter, and of spikes in the batter's box dirt. You can smell the cut grass, the dirt, and the oil of the tar tabs laying on the ground behind the back stop. You can hear the rumble of ice in the metal tubs and the clink and hiss of a soda being pulled from the ice water and uncapped. You remember the sound of someone on the other side of the back stop digging around in a box of Cracker Jacks to find the prize. And you remember what it was like once again, to feel the joy of the game.

It's been quite a while since then and while other memories have faded, it's not hard to remember those sounds and smells from years gone by. They are forever burned into the hearts of every kid who ever picked up a bat and glove.

Kids will be kids and sometimes grown men will still be kids, and it made perfect sense back then. Founding the Jacobus Athletic Association, and later the Jacobus Recreation Association, was serious business, but most who were there at the beginning would probably say that the business part was just something that they had to get out of the way so that they could then go out and get back to playing. In the process of all of that, something unexpected happened and the whole community found the prize.

There have been many hours spent by many individuals who have volunteered their time, effort, and skills to contribute to this project over the years, and "it ain't over" yet.

A ballpark was created back then and a legacy was born. The generations going forward will continue to work and play at this park for as long as these things last, and after that, it will still hopefully live on in stories like this one… but no matter what, it will always be a gift passed down to us from the past. Given to us by those founders who in the end, just wanted a place to play baseball.

ABOUT THE AUTHOR

Doug Arnold is the son of Carl ("Red") and Ellenor Arnold. Born at York Hospital – York, PA., and raised in Jacobus, PA., he was an observer of some of what went on in this book, and sometimes a participant. He is currently employed as a technology consultant and lives in Lancaster, PA.

My Dad, Red Arnold, and the author walking down Main Street in Cooperstown, New York in 2012, toward the Baseball Hall of Fame. (Photo courtesy of my sister Diane.)

Sources

Many thanks to all of the following sources. Without their help there would be no book.

- **My Mom and Dad and brothers and sister**. When I started my research and began asking questions, Mom and Dad created a short document called "The Jacobus Baseball Story", which became part of the framework for a lot of this book. I also recorded a number of hours of audio interviews with my parents, to supplement what was in their document. They helped tremendously with editing and corrections. My brothers and sister have helped with editing, corrections, making suggestions, filling in the blanks, and adding to what I remembered (or didn't) about all of this. Many of the photographs included also came from Mom and Dad's collection

- **The Jacobus Athletic Association Minutes**. My Dad still has the original copy of the minutes, and this was an invaluable aid when doing the research.

- **My uncles Bob, Lee, Ted, and George Arnold**. During recorded interviews, they provided many stories and tall tales, and helped a tremendous amount with editing and filling in the details. They also provided newspaper articles, and my uncle Lee provided a part of his autobiographical material related to all of this. Uncle George also went along with my Dad and I, the first time we discovered the old baseball trophies at the Jacobus Fire Hall.

- **Linette Snyder**. Speaking of the baseball trophies. Many thanks to Linette for twice allowing me access to photograph the trophies in the basement of the Jacobus Fire Hall.

- **Gene and Donna Snyder**. Gene allowed me to photograph his old uniform and jacket, and he and his wife Donna helped with editing and filling in the blanks about many of the names in the Roster Appendix.

- **Sylvia Yarnell (Myers).** Sylvia provided the photos of the 1938 team and field.

- **The York Heritage Trust Library Archives**. Provided many of the news articles used. Thanks to Mr. Albert Rose for showing me the ropes there.

- **The quotes** at the beginning of each chapter have been reprinted, with permission, from **The Gigantic Book of Baseball Quotations**, published by Skyhorse Publishing, Inc,

- **York County Archives**. Those who work there helped me to locate what I needed and provided copies of the deeds.

Appendix A: Purchase of the Property

This is a timeline and summary of the purchase of the Jacobus Community Park property from Mont Smith. It appears that even before the Jacobus Athletic Association was formed in December 1947, the Jacobus Baseball Team had already begun the process of purchasing the new property.

Most of the following information is taken from the Jacobus Athletic Association's meetings minutes.

December 11, 1947 - A motion by Elmer Geiselman, seconded by Bill Hildebrand, was made that we pay Nevin

Smith $280.00 to cover his payment for the Association as the balance of the down payment on the athletic field." (**Author** - I could find no record of what the original down payment was.)

December 28, 1948 - "Decision was made to purchase 35 feet to increase the baseball field from right field to center field. The cost will be $280.00."

(**Author's Note:** It's a little unclear as to the money transactions that took place for the land purchases from Mont Smith. In the Auditor's report from **December 31, 1948** it shows:

Liabilities:
Mortgage held by Mont Smith - $1000.00
Purchase of Land in November 1948- $280.00 (**Author's Note** - this was to extend right field)
Note held by Nevin Smith - $500.00 (**Author's Note** – it appears that some of the local businessmen stepped up to do part of the original financing of the property.)

(**Author's Note** – The transfer of the first deed (that the Author could track down), took place on 7/1/1949 for the sum of $1.00, from Mont Smith and wife to the Jacobus Athletic Association. See the copies of the deeds included in this appendix.)

December 27, 1949 - "A D.R.F Club (**Author** – it looks like D.R.F. stood for "Debt Retirement Fund".) lottery was being conducted by the association, the proceeds of which can be used only to reduce the principal of our mortgage.

February 28, 1950 - The chairman of the D.R.F. Club reported he turned over to the financial secretary $100.00 which is to be used only to reduce our debt on the field.

It was decided on a motion by Sidney Straley seconded by Carroll Hildebrand that we pay the $500.00 note which we've had for two years interest free of which $400.00 was to come out of the treasury and $100.00 which was received from the D.R.F. club. (**Author** – this is probably the note held by Nevin Smith, mentioned in the 1949 Association minutes.)

The president appointed Nevin Smith, Sam Babble, and Carl Folkenroth as a committee to get the title to the ball field. (**Author** – not sure what this means.)

March 28, 1950 – "On a motion by Clark Shearer, seconded by Fred S. Shearer, and carried by voice vote, the Directors of the Jacobus A.A. Inc were given the authority to proceed with the following: "Be it resolved that the Jacobus A.A. In borrowing the sum of one Thousand ($1000.00) Dollars from S.C. Babble of Jacobus, PA and to secure the debt, execute a first mortgage on the Corporation's property located in the Borough of Jacobus which was purchased from Mont Smith and Anna Mary Smith his wife, by deed dated July 1, 1949; the terms of the mortgage shall be for one (1) year with interest at the rate of three (3) percent per annum, payable quarter-annually. The proper officers of the Corporation are hereby authorized ordered and directed to execute the said mortgage and to deliver the same to the Mortgagee upon receipt of the sum of One Thousand ($1000.00) dollars, and said officers are further authorized and directed to pay all necessary expenses incurred thereby".

April 25, 1950 - It was decided to pay Lawyer Rocco for searching title to the field etc. - $31.25

September 20, 1950 - It was decided to pay our loan and interest to Sam Babble, of $1,000.00 plus $7.50 interest.

December 31, 1950 – As shown on the Auditor's report at the end of 1950…

Receipts – "Debt Retirement Fund": $115.85, Loan from S.C. Babble: $1000.00
Expenses – Nevin Smith pay loan: $500.00, Mont Smith, pay mortgage: $1000.00, S.C. Babble, pay mortgage: $1000.00,

loan interest: $30.00

Looks like the total for the original field then, beginning from 1947, came to around ($280.00 + $115.85 + $1000.00 + $500 + $31.35 + $1000.00 + $30.00) = **$2957.10**.

November 19,1952 - It was decided to buy a 385' piece of land from Mont Smith. Cost to be not more than $6.00 per foot. (**Author** – this is the property across Pleasant Avenue from the ball diamond where the basketball court, tennis court, and other facilities are now located.)

December 17, 1952 - The land extension purchase has been agreed to with Mont and Anna Mary Smith. The transaction will be completed in the spring of 1953. In the minutes it is described as "the land opposite to the ball diamond". (**Author** – this is the property across Pleasant Avenue from the ball diamond where the basketball court, tennis court, and other facilities are now located.)

June 24, 1953 - It was agreed that the assoc. will put a down payment on the field, whatever was available, and Mont Smith will hold the deed until we pay the remainder. (**Author** – this is the property across Pleasant Avenue from the ball diamond where the basketball court, tennis court, and other facilities are now located.)

July 15, 1953 - Motion was made that the assoc. pays $1150.00 for the ground purchased from Mont Smith – this amount being half of the price. Motion was carried. (**Author** – this is the property across Pleasant Avenue from the ball diamond where the basketball court, tennis court, and other facilities are now located.) According to the Deed the total price was $2179.00)

There was a discussion on what would be done with the ground being bought. Nothing was decided at this time.

September 16, 1953 - Carl Folkenroth reported $1200.00 was paid on the land we bought from Mont Smith. We still owe $979.00 on this debt.

November 18, 1953 - Arthur Shearer made a motion, seconded by A. P. Falkenstine, that we pay off the land we bought from Month Smith, this year yet. Motion carried.

December 23, 1953 - The President reported that Carl Folkenroth has the check ready to pay the field in full just as soon as Mont Smith comes back from Florida.

April 29, 1954 – On the deed, it was marked that the final payment was made and Mont Smith indicated that it was "Paid in Full"

June 30, 1959 – On this date the property passed from the Jacobus Athletic association to the Jacobus Borough for $1.

3596.

MONT SMITH UX . :
TO :
JACOBUS ATHLETIC ASSOCIATION :

$2.75 FED.REV

THIS DEED, MADE THE First day of July in the year of our Lord one thousand nine hundred forty nine.

BETWEEN Mont Smith and Anna Mary Smith, his wife, of the Borough of Jacobus, York County, Pennsylvania, Grantors, and Jacobus Athletic Association, a non profit corporation, organized and existing under and by virtue of the laws of the Commonwealth of Pennsylvania, having its principal place of business in the Borough of Jacobus, York County, Pennsylvania, Grantee:

WITNESSETH, that in consideration of One ($1.00) Dollars, in hand paid, the receipt whereof is hereby acknowledged, the said grantors do hereby grant and convey to the said grantee,

All that certain tract of land situate and being in the Borough of Jacobus, York County, Pennsylvania, bounded and described as follows, to wit:

BEGINNING at an iron pin on the Northwest corner of Pleasant Avenue and a public road, extending thence along the Western line of said Pleasant Avenue North two (2) degrees East three hundred eighty five (385) feet to an iron pin at other lands of the Grantors hereto; thence along said land North eighty eight (88) degrees West three hundred thirty three and five tenths (333.5) feet to an iron pin on the East side of Franklin Street; thence along the East side of said Franklin Street South five (5) degrees West three hundred sixty six (366) feet to an iron pin on the East side of Franklin Street at corner of property of Paul Decker; thence along property of Paul Decker North eighty six (86) degrees thirty (30) minutes East one hundred fifty six and seventy five one hundredths (156.75) feet to an iron pin; by same South two (2) degrees West sixty (60) feet to an iron pin on the North side of aforesaid public road; thence along the North side of aforesaid public road North eighty one (81) degrees thirty (30) minutes East one hundred eighty seven (187) feet to the place of BEGINNING.

Containing three and seven one hundredths (3.07) acres of land.

Being a part of the same property which Franklin R. Krout and Louisa Krout, his wife, by their deed dated December 21st, A.D. 1922, and recorded in the Office for the Recording of Deeds in and for York County, Pennsylvania, in Deed Book 22-I, page 359, granted and conveyed unto Mont Smith, who joined with his wife, are the grantors hereto. Reference thereto being had will more fully and at large appear.

AND, the said grantors, do hereby covenant and agree to and with the said grantee, that they, the grantors, their heirs, executors and administrators, shall and will warrant generally and forever defend the herein above described premises, with the hereditaments and appurtenances, unto the said grantee, its heirs and assigns, against the said grantors, and against every other person lawfully claiming or who shall hereafter claim the same or any part thereof.

IN WITNESS WHEREOF, said grantors have hereunto set their hands and seals the day and year first above written.

Signed, Sealed and Delivered
in the Presence of
William F. Fry

Mont Smith (SEAL)
Anna Mary Smith (SEAL)

State of Pennsylvania)
: ss.
County of York)

On this, the First day of July, 1949, before me, a Notary Public in and for the said

Page 1 of the original deed transfer. July 1, 1949. (From the York County Archives)

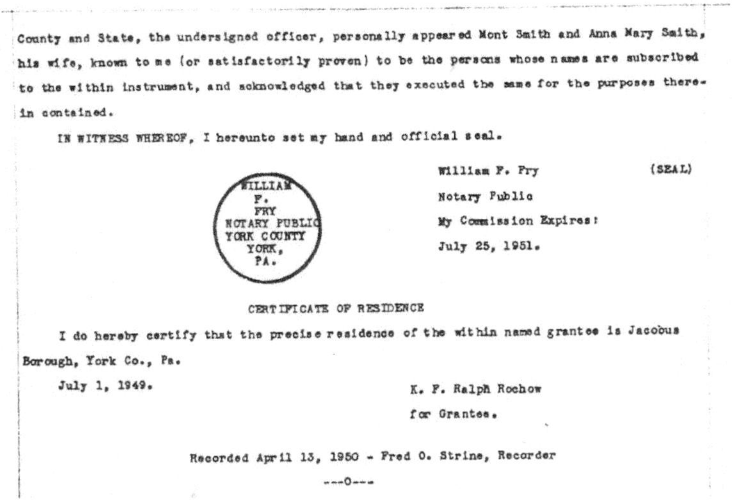

County and State, the undersigned officer, personally appeared Mont Smith and Anna Mary Smith, his wife, known to me (or satisfactorily proven) to be the persons whose names are subscribed to the within instrument, and acknowledged that they executed the same for the purposes therein contained.

IN WITNESS WHEREOF, I hereunto set my hand and official seal.

William F. Fry (SEAL)
Notary Public
My Commission Expires:
July 25, 1951.

CERTIFICATE OF RESIDENCE

I do hereby certify that the precise residence of the within named grantee is Jacobus Borough, York Co., Pa.

July 1, 1949.

K. F. Ralph Rochow
for Grantee.

Recorded April 13, 1950 - Fred O. Strine, Recorder

---0---

Page 2 of the original deed transfer. July 1, 1949. (From the York County Archives)

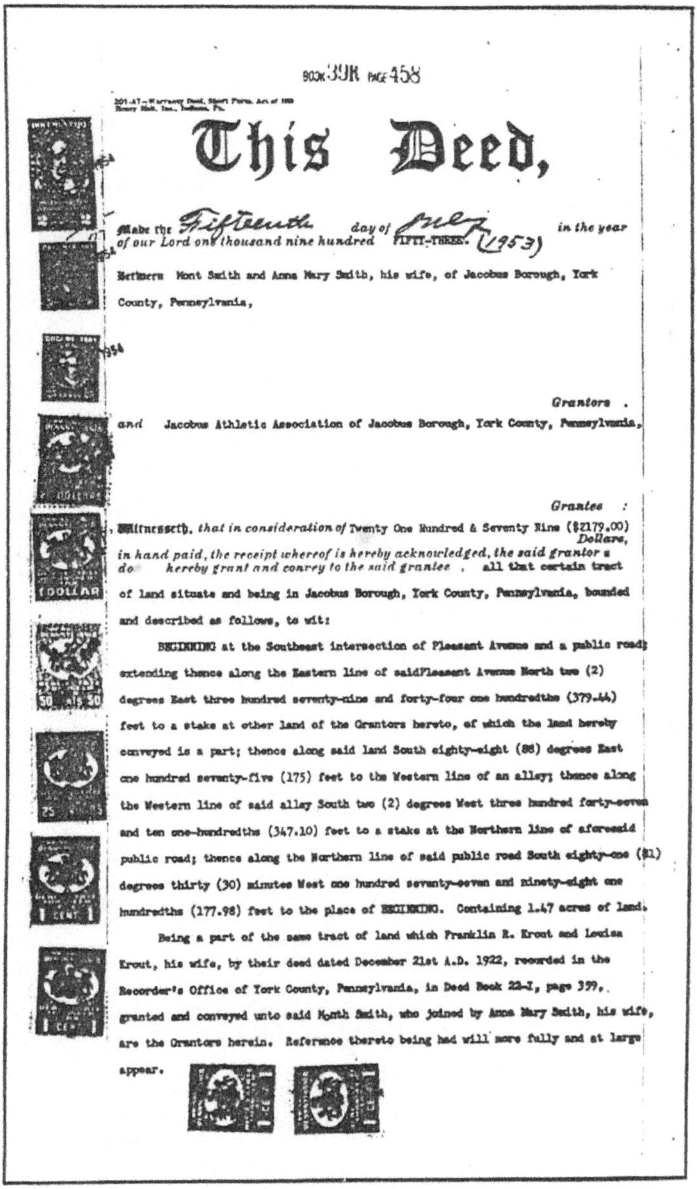

BOOK 39R PAGE 458

This Deed,

Made the Fifteenth day of July in the year of our Lord one thousand nine hundred FIFTY-THREE. (1953)

Between Mont Smith and Anna Mary Smith, his wife, of Jacobus Borough, York County, Pennsylvania,

Grantors .

and Jacobus Athletic Association of Jacobus Borough, York County, Pennsylvania,

Grantee :

Witnesseth, that in consideration of Twenty One Hundred & Seventy Nine ($2179.00) Dollars, in hand paid, the receipt whereof is hereby acknowledged, the said grantor s do hereby grant and convey to the said grantee , all that certain tract of land situate and being in Jacobus Borough, York County, Pennsylvania, bounded and described as follows, to wit:

BEGINNING at the Southeast intersection of Pleasant Avenue and a public road; extending thence along the Eastern line of saidPleasant Avenue North two (2) degrees East three hundred seventy-nine and forty-four one hundredths (379.44) feet to a stake at other land of the Grantors hereto, of which the land hereby conveyed is a part; thence along said land South eighty-eight (88) degrees East one hundred seventy-five (175) feet to the Western line of an alley; thence along the Western line of said alley South two (2) degrees West three hundred forty-seven and ten one-hundredths (347.10) feet to a stake at the Northern line of aforesaid public road; thence along the Northern line of said public road South eighty-one (81) degrees thirty (30) minutes West one hundred seventy-seven and ninety-eight one hundredths (177.98) feet to the place of BEGINNING. Containing 1.47 acres of land.

Being a part of the same tract of land which Franklin R. Krout and Louisa Krout, his wife, by their deed dated December 21st A.D. 1922, recorded in the Recorder's Office of York County, Pennsylvania, in Deed Book 22-I, page 399, granted and conveyed unto said Month Smith, who joined by Anna Mary Smith, his wife, are the Grantors herein. Reference thereto being had will more fully and at large appear.

Page 1 of the deed adding property for the playground and recreation area. July 15th, 1953. (From the York County Archives)

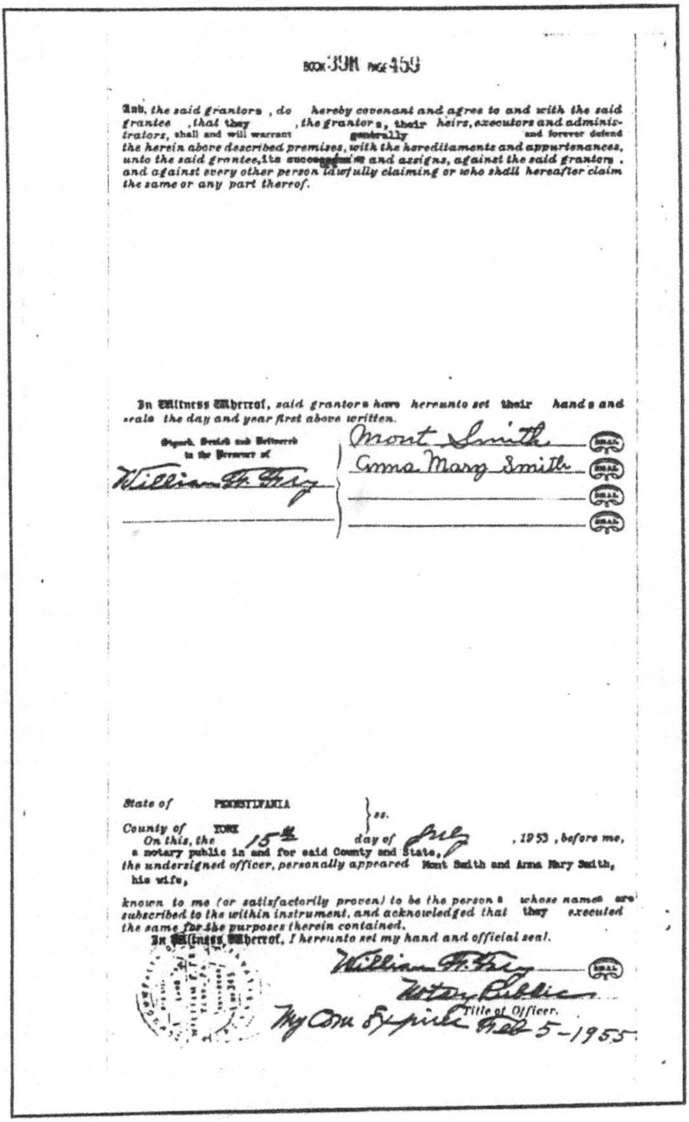

BOOK 39M PAGE 459

And, the said grantors , do hereby covenant and agree to and with the said grantee , that they , the grantors, their heirs, executors and administrators, shall and will warrant generally and forever defend the herein above described premises, with the hereditaments and appurtenances, unto the said grantee, its successors and assigns, against the said grantors . and against every other person lawfully claiming or who shall hereafter claim the same or any part thereof.

In Witness Whereof, said grantors have hereunto set their hands and seals the day and year first above written.

Signed, Sealed and Delivered in the Presence of

William F. Frey

Mont Smith (SEAL)
Anna Mary Smith (SEAL)
(SEAL)
(SEAL)

State of PENNSYLVANIA
County of YORK } ss.

On this, the 15th day of July , 1953 , before me, a notary public in and for said County and State, the undersigned officer, personally appeared Mont Smith and Anna Mary Smith, his wife,

known to me (or satisfactorily proven) to be the persons whose names are subscribed to the within instrument, and acknowledged that they executed the same for the purposes therein contained.

In Witness Whereof, I hereunto set my hand and official seal.

William F. Frey (SEAL)
Notary Public
Title of Officer.
My Com Expires Feb 5-1955

Page 2 of the deed adding property for the playground and recreation area. July 15th, 1953. (From the York County Archives)

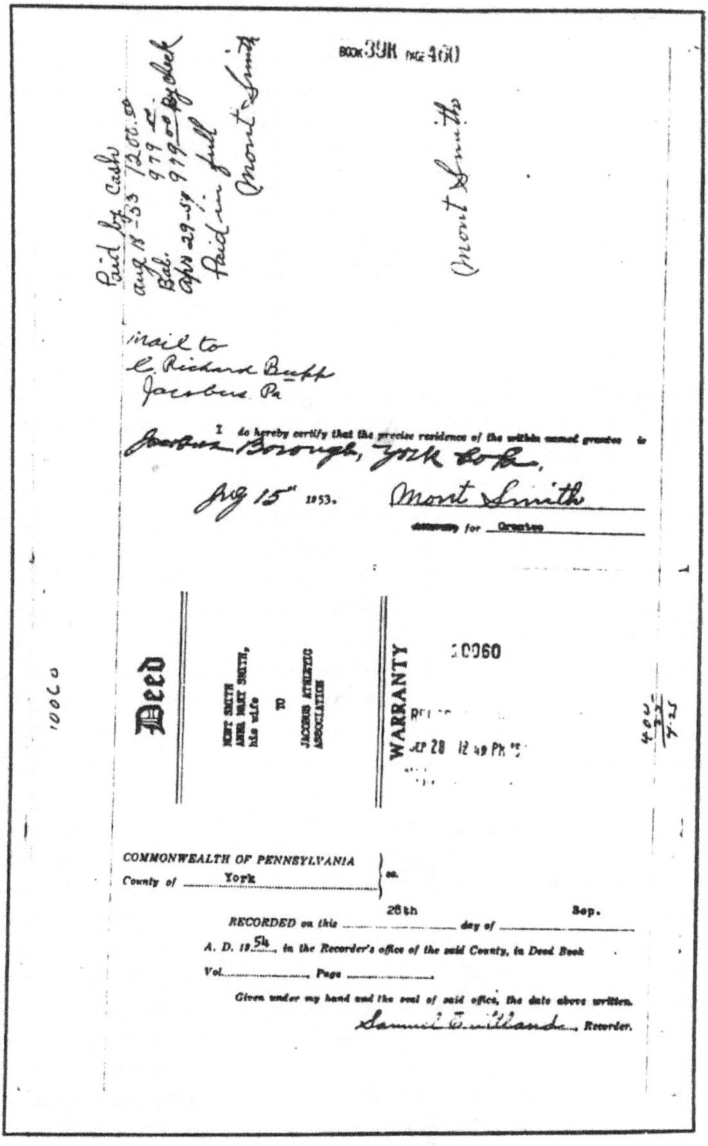

BOOK 39K PAGE 460

Paid by Cash
aug 18-53 7200.00
Bal. 979.00
Apr 29-54 979.00 By check
Paid in full
Mont Smith

Mont Smith

mail to
C. Richard Buff
Jacobus Pa

I do hereby certify that the precise residence of the within named grantee is Jacobus Borough, York Co Pa.

Aug 15" 1953. Mont Smith
Attorney for Grantee

Deed

MONT SMITH
ANNA MARY SMITH,
his wife
TO
JACOBUS ATHLETIC
ASSOCIATION

WARRANTY

10060

COMMONWEALTH OF PENNSYLVANIA
County of York } ss.

RECORDED on this 28th day of Sep.
A. D. 19 54, in the Recorder's office of the said County, in Deed Book
Vol. .... Page ....
Given under my hand and the seal of said office, the date above written.
Samuel E. Gillands, Recorder.

Page 3 of the deed adding property for the playground and recreation area. July 15th, 1953. (From the York County Archives)

75

VOL 48H PAGE 98

321-T—Deed from Corporation to Individual or Corp.
Henry Hall, Inc., Indiana, Pa.

8348

This Indenture,

MADE THE Thirtieth *day of* June *in the year of our Lord one thousand nine hundred* and fifty-nine (1959).

BETWEEN JACOBUS ATHLETIC ASSOCIATION, a non-profit corporation organized and existing under and by virtue of the laws of the Commonwealth of Pennsylvania, having its principal place of business in Jacobus Borough, York County, Pennsylvania,

--- GRANTOR,

- a n d -

THE BOROUGH OF JACOBUS, a municipal corporation located in York County, Pennsylvania,

--- GRANTEE:

WITNESSETH, that the said Jacobus Athletic Association,

for and in consideration of the sum of ONE ($1.00) DOLLAR, ------------------

lawful money of the United States of America, unto it *well and truly paid by the said* The Borough of Jacobus,
at and before the sealing and delivery of these presents, the receipt whereof is hereby acknowledged, has *granted, bargained, sold, aliened, enfeoffed, released and confirmed, and by these presents* does *grant, bargain, sell, alien, enfeoff, release and confirm unto the said* The Borough of Jacobus, its successors *and assigns,*

ALL those certain described two (2) tracts of land situate and being in Jacobus Borough, York County, Pennsylvania, bounded and limited as follows, to wit:

TRACT NO. 1: BEGINNING at an iron pin on the Northwest corner of Pleasant Avenue and a public road; extending thence along the Western line of said Pleasant Avenue North two (2) degrees East, three hundred eighty-five (385) feet to an iron pin at lands now or formerly of Mont Smith; thence along said land North eighty-eight (88) degrees West, three hundred thirty-three and five-tenths (333.5) feet to an iron pin on the East side of Franklin Street; thence along the East side of said Franklin Street South five (5) degrees West, three hundred sixty-six (366) feet to an iron pin on the East side of Franklin Street at corner of property now or formerly of Paul Decker; thence along property now or formerly of Paul Decker North eighty-six (86) degrees, thirty (30) minutes East, one hundred fifty-six and seventy-five one-hundredths (156.75) feet to an iron pin; thence by the same South two (2) degrees West, sixty (60) feet to an iron pin on the North side of the aforesaid public road; thence along the North side of the aforesaid public road North eighty-one (81) degrees, thirty (30) minutes East, one hundred eighty-seven (187) feet to the place of BEGINNING. Containing three and seven one-hundredths (3.07) acres of land.

IT BEING the same property which Mont Smith and Anna Mary Smith, his wife, by their deed dated July 1, 1949, and recorded in the Recorder's Office for York County, Pennsylvania in Deed Book 35-J, page 142, granted and conveyed unto Jacobus Athletic Association, GRANTOR herein.

TRACT NO. 2: BEGINNING at the Southeast intersection of Pleasant Avenue and a public road; extending thence along the Eastern line of said Pleasant Avenue North two (2) degrees East, three hundred

Page 1 of the final deed transfer to the Borough of Jacobus. June 30th^h, 1959. (From the York County Archives)

VOL 48H PAGE 99

seventy-nine and forty-four one-hundredths (379.44) feet to a stake at land now or formerly of Mont Smith; thence along said land South eighty-eight (88) degrees East, one hundred seventy-five (175) feet to the Western line of an alley; thence along the Western line of said alley South two (2) degrees West, three hundred forty-seven and ten one-hundredths (347.10) feet to a stake at the Northern line of the aforesaid public road; thence along the Northern line of said public road South eighty-one (81) degrees, thirty (30) minutes West, one hundred seventy-seven and ninety-eight one-hundredth (177.98) feet to the place of BEGINNING. Containing one and forty-seven one-hundredths (1.47) acres of land.

IT BEING the same property which Mont Smith and Anna Mary Smith, his wife, by their deed dated July 15, 1953, and recorded in said Recorder's Office in Deed Book 39-R, page 458, granted and conveyed unto Jacobus Athletic Association, GRANTOR herein.

This deed is executed and delivered pursuant to authority contained in a resolution duly adopted at a meeting of the members of the Grantor corporation held May 3, 1959, duly called for the purpose of considering the transfer of the real estate of the corporation.

UNDER AND SUBJECT, NEVERTHELESS, to the condition which is made a part of the consideration for this conveyance, that the land hereby granted shall always be used as a public playground and shall not be used for any other purpose; and the Grantee, for itself, its successors and assigns, agrees to and with the Grantor, its successors and assigns, that said condition shall be a covenant running with the land and that in any deed of conveyance of said premises or any part thereof, to any person or persons, said condition shall be incorporated in such deed or deeds of conveyance as full as the same is contained in this indenture.

Page 2 of the final deed transfer to the Borough of Jacobus. June 30th^h, 1959. (From the York County Archives)

VOL 48H PAGE 100

TOGETHER with all and singular *ways, waters, water-courses, rights, liberties, privileges, hereditaments and appurtenances whatsoever thereunto belonging, or in anywise appertaining, and the reversions and remainders, rents, issues and profits thereof; and all the estate, right, title, interest, property, claim and demand whatsoever, of* Jacobus Athletic Association *in law, equity, or otherwise howsoever, of, in and to the same and every part thereof,*

TO HAVE AND TO HOLD the said hereinbefore described *hereditaments and premises hereby granted or mentioned and intended so to be, with the appurtenances, unto the said* The Borough of Jacobus, its successors *and assigns, to and for the only proper use and behoof of the said* The Borough of Jacobus, its successors *and assigns forever.*

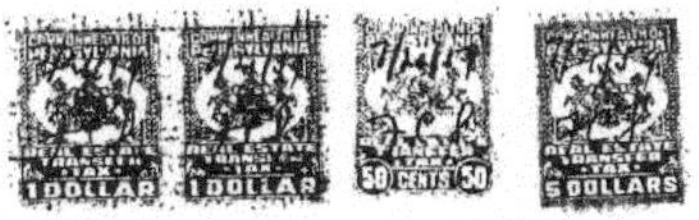

And the said Jacobus Athletic Association *does by these presents, covenant, grant and agree, to and with the said* The Borough of Jacobus, its successors *and assigns, that* it, *the said* Jacobus Athletic Association *all and singular the hereditaments and premises herein above described and granted or mentioned and intended so to be, with the appurtenances, unto the said* The Borough of Jacobus, its successors *and assigns, against* it, *the said* Jacobus Athletic Association, *and against all and every* other *person or persons whomsoever lawfully claiming or to claim the same or any part thereof, shall and will* G e n e r a l l y *warrant and forever defend.*

IN WITNESS WHEREOF, the said JACOBUS ATHLETIC ASSOCIATION, *has caused this Indenture to be signed in its corporate name by its President,* ~~*and has caused to be affixed hereunto the common and corporate seal of the said corporation*~~*, attested by its Secretary, the day and year first above written.*

JACOBUS ATHLETIC ASSOCIATION
By Fred C. Shearer
President.

Attest:
Barry Shearer
Secretary.

JUL 21 1959
Date
York Imperial School District
Realty Transfer Tax
Amount of Tax – $ 7.50
Received Payment
Luther H. Yohe
Recorder Deeds, Collector

Page 3 of the final deed transfer to the Borough of Jacobus. June 30th^h, 1959. (From the York County Archives)

VOL. 48H PAGE 101

State of PENNSYLVANIA
County of YORK } ss.

On this, the thirtieth day of June, 1959, before me, the undersigned officer, personally appeared FRED C. SHEARER, who acknowledged himself to be the President of JACOBUS ATHLETIC ASSOCIATION, a corporation, and that he as such President, being authorized to do so, executed the foregoing instrument for the purposes therein contained by signing the name of the corporation by himself as President.

In witness whereof, I hereunto set my hand and official seal.

Carl J. Folkenroth
Notary Public, York, York County
My Commission Expires August 28, 19..
Title of Officer.

CARL J. FOLKENROTH NOTARY PUBLIC SEAL

CERTIFICATE OF RESIDENCE

I do hereby certify that the precise residence of the within named grantee is Jacobus Borough, Pa.

1959.

Paul E. Stein
Attorney for grantee

008348

8348

Deed

JACOBUS ATHLETIC ASSOCIATION, a non-profit corporation,

- to -

THE BOROUGH OF JACOBUS, a municipal corporation.

RECORDED — PAID
JUL 21 10 46 AM '59
RECORDER OF DEEDS OFFICE
YORK, YORK COUNTY, PA.

450

State of Penna.
County of York } ss.

RECORDED on this 21st day of July A. D. 19 59, in the Recorder's Office of said County, in Deed Book Vol. 48-H, Page 98

Given under my hand and the seal of the said office, the date above written.

Luther N. Yohe, Recorder.

Page 4 of the final deed transfer to the Borough of Jacobus. June 30th^h, 1959. (From the York County Archives)

Appendix B: Jacobus Athletic Association Minutes

Here are extracts from the Jacobus Athletic Association minutes from December 1947 through April 1962. It's interesting to see some of the details of what went on at these meetings.

December, 1947

"Baseball Team meetings were held in the basement of Clete Innerst's Equipment Garage."

The group decided to have an Election Board to oversee the selection of the first officers' and directors for the Athletic Association. "(The Election Board was something designated in the charter. The election Board was in charge of elections and nominations and voting.) "The members selected for the Election Board were: Ken Keiser, Don Rohrbaugh and Carl "Red" Arnold. Nominations were held and the first elected officers were - President: Ralph Innerst; Vice President: Preston Hershner; Secretary: Sid Straley; Assistant Secretary: Rich Arnold; and Treasurer: Nevin Smith; Business Managers: Carroll Hildebrand and Paul Smith. Others involved in the election were – Carl Folkenroth and Earl Hildebrand.

The first elected Board of Directors' were: A. P. Falkenstine; C.L. Innerst; Howard Olp; Elmer Geiselman and Nevin Smith."

"The Court of Common Pleas of York County granted the Jacobus Athletic Association's Charter as a non-profit organization.

A motion by Elmer Geiselman, seconded by Bill Hildebrand, was made that we pay Nevin Smith $280.00 to cover his payment for the Association as the balance of the down payment on the athletic field."

A motion was also made at this board meeting to have C. L. Innerst grade the athletic field as soon as possible.

January 6, 1948

"All assets of the Jacobus Baseball Team treasury contained $520.04. This amount was then turned over to the Jacobus Athletic Association."

January 27, 1948

"Secretary reported $100.00 in receipts from donations. Balance in Treasury was $620.04. It was decided to apply to the Southern York County League, the Twilight League and the Greater York County League. Preferences would be as listed."

February 24, 1948

"Treasurer reported balance in treasury: $321.89. 30 members present. It was reported that the Southern and Twilight Leagues were both filled. The Greater League did not respond yet. Ralph Innerst was appointed Manager of the baseball team for 1948. The By-Laws, after discussions from December, 1947 to January, 1948 were approved."

Membership fee to the Association was $2.00. Dues were $1.00 per year.

There was an ongoing discussion to try and get in to the Greater League and to better the league by having better league records, etc.

"Paul Smith moved that the Executive Committee be given permission to build bleachers and other spectator and player facilities as needed. Seconded by Junior Keeney."

W. H. Hildebrand was appointed and accepted (with some hesitation) as the first grounds keeper of the new field.

"Red Arnold received steel pipes to make the back-stop, donated by Ben Franklin/Jacobus Plastics, Inc.

Paul Smith moved, seconded by Sid Straley, that whatever supplies and equipment were necessary for the upcoming season, be purchased.

Other members that were in attendance other than the above Officers were Carroll Hildebrand, Clete Innerst, Clair Smith, Harry Keiser, Karl Smith, Sterling Myers, Caleb Ferree, Herb Geiselman, Arthur Shearer and Clarke Shearer.

After discussions, the Association decided to add a second team. Preparations, League and Manager will follow at a future meeting."

March 30, 1948

"Nevin Smith reported the estimate to build bleachers will be around $600.00."

New members voted into the association were: S. C. Meyers, Caleb Ferree, Herbert Geiselman, and Arthur Shearer.

"It was reported the first team will continue in the Greater League.

It was also reported that the Jacobus second team will be in the newly formed Western Baseball League. Preston Hershner was named to be manager of the second team. Members of the second team will include Perry Innerst, Jr., Clarke Shearer, Richard Bupp, Bob Falkenstine Lee Arnold, Vernon Geiselman, Red Arnold, Amos Warfel, Rich Arnold, Gerry Snyder, Gerald Schrum, Roy Warfel, Charlie Smith and Dale Innerst. Steve Hershner was designated as bat boy."

An appeal was made to all members to turn out to help get the field in shape for the coming season.

April 27th, 1948

$500.00 was borrowed to pay bills contracted in connection with construction of the bleachers on the athletic field.

Advertising space on the game scorecards had been sold for $362.50.

A treasury balance of $835.47 was reported.

15 more applicants for membership were approved. (Names were not noted.)

"It was decided to buy (12) pair of pants for the Western League team; (36) caps were purchased for both the Greater

League team and the Western League team - so everyone has a cap and that the caps in both leagues matched. Also, everyone got "J's" for their cap, but each must see that it gets put on.

It was decided to have a Committee for the new field dedication ceremony. Appointed to serve were Bill Hildebrand, A. P. Falkenstine and Elmer Geiselman. This will take place at the Opening Day of the Season."

May 25th, 1948

The committee appointed to arrange for a dedication ceremony for the field reported incomplete plans.

The board decided not to purchase insurance on either the players or spectators.

Six new applications for membership were approved. (No names available.)

"Six (6) members were notified they still owed dues for 1948"

There was discussion about some field equipment that had not yet been procured – a batter's screen for batting practice, the score board, forms for chalk-lining the batter's box and coach's boxes. No decisions about this equipment were made.

There was a discussion about some parts of the field equipment which had not yet been procured – batter's screen for batting practice, the scoreboard, and forms for chalk-lining the batter's box and coaches' boxes. Nothing else was done about it at that time.

June 1948 – No meeting of the association was held in June.

July 27th, 1948

The treasury balance was $232.31 as of July 10th, 1948.

Two applications for membership were approved. (No names available.)

Two people were removed due to non-payment of dues.

"It was decided to buy twelve (12) pair of stockings for the first team (Greater League). It was mentioned that more needed to be done to smooth the infield." No definite line of action was decided upon.

August 31st, 1948

The treasurer reported a profit of $184.00 from the Festival held on August 14th. Balance in the treasury was $540.25.

Five applications for membership were approved. (No names available.)

Talk continued about improving the field but no action was taken.

September 28, 1948

A balance of $504.08 was reported as of September 15th, 1948.

"It was decided to add ground in left field, plow and plant grass. Bill Hildebrand was appointed to develop a bake sale to help raise funds for the teams. "

October 1948

No meeting due to a banquet being held at that time.

November 23, 1948

Proceeds of the bake sale were $66.00. Thanks to W.H. Hildebrand was given for that.

Treasury balance was $722.10.

More mention of the condition of the ball field but "as usual" nothing was decided.

An amendment to the By Laws was made regarding the appointment of business managers of the various teams.

New nominations for officers for 1949:

President – Ralph Innerst, Preston Hershner, LeRoy Myers, Herbert Geiselman
Secretary – Carl Folkenroth, Rich Arnold. Sidney Straley
Treasurer – Curtis Darr, Nevin Smith
Directors – A.P. Falkenstine, Elmer Geiselman, Howard Olp, C. L. Innerst, W.G. Darr, C. C. Lehman, Wm Geiselman, W.H. Hildebrand, Melvin Keener, Samuel Babble, Karl Smith, Kenneth Keiser, Jesse Keeney, Clair F. Smith, Russel Shearer, Donald Rohrbaugh, Edward Ferree, Richard Bupp
Business Manager – 1st Team – Carroll Hildebrand, Wm Klein
Business Manager – 2nd Team – Carl D. Arnold, Stanley Kohr

December 28, 1948

Receipts for the month were $10.00, expenses of $305.80, and a treasury balance of $426.30.

Ground was purchased for the ball field, costing $252.00. (Assumption is that this was top soil and ground for repairs.) This caused an "extremely interesting and somewhat heated discussion out of which emerged exactly nothing."

"Decision was made to purchase 35 feet to increase the baseball field from right field to center field. The cost will be $280.00."

"The cost of prizes for a raffle held the previous September was donated by C.L. Innerst, leading to a "rising vote of thanks to Mr. Innerst".

"The Auditors' appointed for the year were Carl Folkenroth, Richard Bupp and Red Arnold."

The Election Committee appointed were: Ben Franklin, Earl Hildebrand and Clarke Shearer.

"After the votes were counted the following were elected: President, Herb Geiselman – Vice President: Ralph Innerst – Secretary: Carl Folkenroth – Assistant Secretary: Sid Straley – Treasurer: Nevin Smith."

Directors: Clete Innerst, A. P. Falkenstine, Sam Babble, Howard Olp, and Clair Smith.

At this point in time, the mortgage ($1000.00) is held by Mont Smith and the association still has a note owed to Nevin Smith for $500.00" Refer to the following Auditors report documents:

The Jacobus Athletic Association Inc.
Auditor's Report Dec. 31, 1948

Receipts		Expenditures	
Bal. on hand Beg yr	264.79	Athletic Equipment	647.20
Membership Fees	190.00	Field Equipment	8.70
Dues for 1948	93.00	Field Bldg + Stands	1094.72
Loan on Note	500.00	Fixtures of 1947 Club	40.50
Donations for 1948	331.25	Payment on Field	700.00
Gate Receipts 1st team	686.81	Concessions	510.85
" " 2nd team	222.27	Festival	655.80
Festival	824.~~45~~ 50	Raffle	393.00
Raffle	895.45	Scorecards printed	99.50
Scorecard Advertising	362.00	Administration	77.7[illegible]
Bakesale	66.00	Interest	36.3[illegible]
Greater League Refund	33.37	Field Maint + Improv.	302.00
Eastern League Refund	21.90	Umpires 1st team	150.00
State Refund on Bleachers	20.00	Umpires 2nd team	107.00
Concessions	848.24	League Exp. 1st team	25.9[illegible]
Sale of Caps + Letters	13.80	League " 2nd team	25.0[illegible]
		Foul Balls Ret'd 1st team	9.1[illegible]
		" " " 2nd team	4.60
		Banquet	71.10
		Total	4959.08
		Bal. in Treasury	414.30
Total	5373.38	Grand Total	5373.3[illegible]

Liabilities:

Mortgage held by Mort Smith	1000.00	
purchase of land November 1948	280.00	1280.00
Note held by [illegible] Smith		500.00
Accounts Payable		6.75

Following are the original by-laws for the Jacobus Athletic Association:

BY-LAWS

OF

THE JACOBUS ATHLETIC ASSOCIATION

__Article__ 1 The name of this Organization shall be "THE JACOBUS ATHLETIC ASSOCIATION"

__Article__ 2 The purpose of this organization is to promote athletic sports and events, such as baseball and other sports, and the ownership and maintainance of facilities for conducting and promoting such sports.

__Article__ 3

Section 1 The privelege of applying for membership will be extended to all persons.

2 Applications for membership must be approved by a majority of the members attending the regular meeting of the Association.

3 Membership fee must accompany any application for membership; such fee will be returned to the applicant in the event that this application is rejected.

4 The membership fee will be Two Dollars ($2.00)

5 The dues will be One Dollar ($1.00) per year, payable on January 1st. of the year, and not later than April 30th. All members will be notified of dues over-due before being dropped from membership in the Association.

__Article__ 4

Section 1 The officers of the Association shall be a President; Vice-president, secretary, assistant secretary, treasurer and five directors. These officers and directors will be the Executive Committee of the Association.

2 The Executive Committee will be the nominating committee and will, before the November meeting of each year, nominate at least two (2) members for candidacy to each office. These nominations of the nominating committee will be read at the November meeting, at which time members may make any additional nominations.

3 No member may be nominated for, or elected to, more than one (1) elective office at any one time. This section will become effective on January 1, 1949.

4 The officers of the Association will be elected by ballot vote at each regular December meeting, and will continue in office until the installation of new officers at the first regular meeting following the election. The candidate for President receiving the second highest number of votes will be the vice-president, and the candidate for secretary receiving the second highest number of votes for that office will be the assistant secretary.

page 2

Section 5 Any vacancy which may occur in the Executive Committee will be filled by appointment by the Executive Committee.

6 A vacancy will occur in the Executive Committee when any member of the Executive Committee fails to attend three meetings of the Executive Committee in succession without good cause. Interpretation of the term "good cause" will be left to the discretion of the Executive Committee.

7 Any member in good standing shall be eligible for election to any office.

Article 5 The duties of the officers shall be as follows:

THE PRESIDENT

1 Will preside at all meetings of both the membership and the Executive Committee.

2 Will appoint all committees. The first named person on each committee, automatically being the chairman of that committee.

3 He will sign all vouchers.

THE VICE-PRESIDENT

1 He will assume all the duties of the president in the absence of the president.

THE SECRETARY

1 R He shall take the minutes of all meetings of both membership and the executive committee.

2 He will notify all members of any arrearages.

3 He will present all bills and handle all correspondence pertaining to business of the association.

4 He will receive all money and forward it to the Treasurer immediately.

5 He will sign all vouchers.

6 He will, at the end of his term in office, turn over to his successor in good order all records, books, papers, documents and all other possessions of the association in his possession.

THE ASSISTANT SECRETARY

1 ~~He will assist the secretary in any manner.~~

page 3

THE TREASURER

1 He will care for and be responsible for all monies belong-ing to the association.

2 He will be bonded in any amount which the Executive Committee specifies.

3 He will give the secretary a receipt for all money turned in to him by the secretary.

4 He will, at the end of his term in office, turn over to his successor, in good order, all records, books, papers, documents, and all other possessions of the association in his possession.

THE EXECUTIVE COMMITTEE

1 They will be empowered to buy and sell real estate and property, and to borrow money, only with the approval of the membership; and to engage in any other financial transactions not exceeding Fifty Dollars ($50.00) in any one month without approval of the membership.

2 They will appoint the managers of all athletic teams. Each manager will appoint his own assistants.

Article 6
Section 1 Meetings of the Association will be held regularly on the last Tuesday of each month.

2 A special meeting may be called at any time by the President, and must be called by him on written petition of five (5) members of the Executive Committee.

Article 7 The President will, in December, appoint a committee of three (3) to audit all books. This committee shall make its report to the membership at the January meeting.

Article 8 These by-laws must be amended, if that is desired, only at a regular meeting of the Association, two-thirds of the members present concurring. Amendments must be presented to the meeting in writing and must be held over one (1) month before being voted upon.

Article 9 Order of meetings will be as follows:

1- Call to order
2- Roll call of officers
3- Reading of the minutes of the previous meeting.
4- Reports of officers and committees
5- Proposition and election of new members
6- Unfinished business
7- New business.

Following is a sample from Jacobus Athletic Association stationary discussing uniforms to be purchased:

Jacobus Athletic Asso., Inc.

JACOBUS, PENNA.

Grove showed variety of jackets.

Gray jacket trimmed in maroone – J maroone on front – Baseball – maroone & white letters snaps & knit collar.

January, 25 1949

Meeting held at C.L. Innerst's garage. President Ralph Innerst presiding.

George Keeney Jr. and Sid Straley attended a meeting of the York Co. Twilight League to see if there were any current openings, but it was reported that there were no berth's open at the moment but would be considered for a future opening.

The auditor's report from 1948 was presented. A copy of this report can be found in the previous pages.

Newly elected members were installed to their elected offices – Herbert Geiselman, President; Ralph Innerst, Vice President; Carl Folkenroth, Secretary; Sidney Straley, Assistant Secretary; M. Nevin Smith, Treasurer; and A. P. Falkenstine, Howard Olp, C.L. Innerst, Clair F. Smith, and Samuel Babble as members of the Executive Committee. Also, Carl D. Arnold as business manager of the second team (Western League). Possible business manager for the first team – Carroll Hildebrand was not present and so was not installed.

Possibility of a membership drive was suggested – "a meeting open to the public at which movies of the 1948 World Series and other pictures pertaining to baseball would be shown."

An amendment was proposed and passed stating that anyone under 16 years does not have any Association voting privileges. In addition, anyone under 16 years can become a member and attend regular meetings if they pay the yearly dues of $1.00.

A membership committee was appointed. Richard Bupp, Sam Babble, Karl Smith, A. P. Falkenstine and Carl Folkenroth to serve on the committee.

A motion was made and approved to try to get in the Southern York County League for 1949 (The first team was dissatisfied with the Greater York Co. League).

The second team will stay in the Western League. Red Arnold was appointed Business Manager for the Western League team.

It was decided to spend $200.00 to have Clete Innerst improve the condition of the baseball field by adding ground, grading, dragging, and spreading new lawn seed and fertilizer.

February, 22 1949

Meeting held at C.L. Innerst's garage. President Herbert Geiselman presiding. The treasurer reported receipts for the month $45.00, expenses $6.75, leaving a balance of $452.55 in the treasury.

Membership applications were passed out to the members and everyone was asked to participate in the membership drive.

Herbert Geiselman gave a report on the Greater League Meeting. Nevin Smith gave a report on the Southern League meeting, stating they have accepted our 1st team in the league. Therefore, holding a berth in two leagues. Herbert Geiselman said that he would notify the Greater League of our withdrawal.

Because there were some problems finding a business manager for both of the baseball teams, the By Laws were amended to discontinue electing a business manager for each team. "A committee of three shall be appointed by the Executive Committee to be business managers for all baseball teams sponsored by the Jaccobus Athletic Association."

Contracts were given to players and are available for anyone interested in playing ball for the Jacobus AA Inc.

An invitation was extended to change over to the Southern League for the first team. Offer was accepted.

Nine (9) new members were added. No names listed. It was decided sixteen (16) years of age will be required to be a member."

March 8, 1949

Special meeting of the Jacobus AA Inc was held at C. L. Innerst garage. President Herbert Geiselman presiding.

The treasurer reported no receipts, expenses $25.00 Western League, 15.00 Southern League forfeit money, and $5.00 for treasurer's bond, leaving a balance $407.55 in the treasury.

Reported that 20 new member applications, signed up at the World Series movie on Saturday March 5th…

Motion made to show movies again on 3/19/1949 and carried.

Nevin Smith gave a report on the Southern League Meeting… league decided that all clubs must have their ground rules in written form, available for umpires before game time.

No manager yet picked for the second team.

Main topic for the evening was the "Cooperative Compensation Plan". **(Author – Not sure what this is.)** The plan was adopted by the executive committee as the policy of the association in the regards to the players on the first team.

March 29, 1949

Meeting was held in the C. L. Innerst's garage. President Herbert Geiselman presiding.

The treasurer reported expenditures - $15.00 + $10.00 forfeit money, $5.00 treasurer bond which was donated to the club. $50.26 for refreshments etc. sold at the movies, $6.50 for post cards, receipts $101.00 from dues and fees, leaving a balance of $452.79 in the treasury.

Motions were made to purchase necessary equipment and supplies to run the ball clubs. Also, purchasing hats for whoever needs them.

(**Author** – it appears from the minutes that recently the second team had moved to the City County League.) A report on the City County League was heard by Sid Straley, substituting for Carl D. Arnold. He said that the league has adopted the Goldsmith ball and no forfeit money was paid as yet (**Author** – Not positive what "forfeit money" was as mentioned many times in the notes from the minutes. My guess is that you paid this to the league in case you decided to leave the league at a later time.)

Discussions were held on purchasing an insurance plan for the first team. Milt Baker will attend to present information for discussion on insurance.

The Club added (30) new members. Membership now includes (144) members. A report on the possibilities of the City-County League was made.

Bill Kline was appointed Business Manager Chairman. Earl Hildebrand and Red Arnold will serve as Business Managers for the second team. A Manager for the second team is still needed.

Les Lehman was appointed as first team Manager. Some complaints were aired about his price.

A discussion about season and patron tickets was dropped for this season.

April 26, 1949

Meeting was held in the C. L. Innerst's garage. President Herbert Geiselman presiding.

The treasurer reported receipts for the month $238.38, expenditures $102.51, leaving a balance of $560.11 in the treasury.

Sid Straley reported progress on the Score-Card and turned over to the secretary $403.50. (**Author** – at this point this is the first mention of the score card that I'm aware of.)

It was decided first aid kits for each team be obtained or replenished, whichever needed, and new bases be purchased for the ball field.

Curtis Darr was working on the score board.

Charlie Bupp and Sam Babble volunteered to help in field maintenance. Discussion was held regarding a track meet for May 12th (**Author** – it appears that the track meet was a money raising event, including tickets). Help will be needed to prepare and run the meet. Discussion was held regarding a Baseball for Boys team. Clair Smith volunteered to install home plate for game use.

May 31, 1949

Meeting was held in the C. L. Innerst's garage. President Herbert Geiselman presiding.

The treasurer reported $396.38 in the treasury.

Sid Straley gave a financial report on the May Day Festival and Track meet.

There was a question brought up about the insurance coverage on the ball players. Bill Klein then read the policy stating a 10-dollar deducible of which the club pays the first 10 dollars in any accident which might occur. This was misinterpreted when the policy was purchased.

Approval was made to purchase grass seed to sow the outfield – on this project – Howard Olp, Charles Bupp, and Carroll Hildebrand.

Four (4) new members were added. Picnic Committee held discussions. Bill Kline led discussions on insurance coverage. The second team decided to move to the City-County League. (**Author** – my Dad may have added this based on his memory of events.) Umpires for the team will be handled by the Board of Directors.

A "push limer" will be purchased to place the foul lines on the field. Ralph Innerst was appointed as Chairman of the Picnic Committee. He will appoint people as needed.

June 28, 1949

Meeting was held in the C. L. Innerst's garage. President Herbert Geiselman presiding.

The treasurer reported receipts for the month as $822.71, expenditures $736.48, leaving a total balance of $606.49 in the treasury.

It was decided to pay C. L. Innerst his bill which we have received for mower and work on the diamond.

Discussions were held on hiring another pitcher for the first team, because of several rain cancelled games has tightened the schedule. The Board of Directors will look at hiring a pitcher.

July 26, 1949

Meeting was held in the C. L. Innerst's garage. President Herbert Geiselman presiding.

The treasury reports receipts for the month as $809.27, expenditures $768.53, leaving a balance of $862.30 in the treasury.

City County League was having an Allstar game August 7th, 1949.

The second team reported the City-County League would like to hold an All-Star Game. The Association's Picnic will be held August 13th in Hartman's Grove. The purchase of a new home plate and pitcher's mound was approved.

August 30, 1949

Meeting was held in the C. L. Innerst's garage. President Herbert Geiselman presiding.

The treasurer reported receipts as $869.36, expenditures $698.21, leaving a total balance of $819.14 in the treasury.

It was decided because of crowd movement between the dugout and backstop, a chain will be placed in both areas. Picnic profits were $52.06 (**Author** – receipts $490.00, expenses $437.94). Raffle profits were $87.20 (**Author** – receipts $236.95, expenses $150.75).

September 27, 1949

Meeting was held in the C. L. Innerst's garage. President Herbert Geiselman presiding.

The treasurer reported receipts for the month of $1479.16, expenses $461.08, leaving a total of $1693.92 in the treasury.

It was decided to have a banquet for the ball teams.

More discussions on leveling and seeding the ball field. C. L. Innerst to get a few bids.

A bouquet of flowers was sent to Clint Lehman because of sickness (**Author** – he was in the hospital). Cost not less than $5.00. Howard Olp will handle.

(Author) – no meeting in the record for October.

November 22, 1949

Meeting was held in the C. L. Innerst's garage. President Herbert Geiselman presiding.

Treasurer was absent so no treasurer report.

Letter from the US treasury asking for copies of the By-Laws and Articles of Incorporation of the Association. Secretary to attend to this.

The Officers and Board of Directors made adjustments (**Author** – amendment number 4) to the By-Laws to meet Federal Requirements. Rebate check of $46.65 was received from the Southern York County League (**Author** – forfeit money and share of the profits from the Allstar game.)

December 27, 1949

Meeting was held in the C. L. Innerst's garage. President Herbert Geiselman presiding.

Amendment number four to the By-Laws was re-read and approved.

January 31, 1950

Meeting was held in the C. L. Innerst's garage. Vice President Jesse Keeney presiding.

The report on the movies shown January 21st was heard by Sid Straley at which was shown pictures of the 1949 World Series and a serial on Snuffy Smith. Receipts for this affair were $48.85, expenses $52.08, goods left over to sell at the next movie $11.42, showing a loss of $3.73 until we sell the goods.

The basketball request to the Jacobus Fire Company will be put on hold till the new Fire Hall is completed (**Author** – next year, 1951).

After discussion, it was decided to again sponsor a second team regardless of what league was entered.

February 28, 1950

Meeting was held in the C. L. Innerst's garage. President Herbert Geiselman presiding.

The chairman of the D.R.F. Club (**Author** – it looks like D.R.F. stood for "Debt Retirement Fund".) reported he turned over to the financial secretary $100.00 which is to be used only to reduce our debt on the field.

The new treasurer reported that he had received from the old treasurer $569.49 which was in the bank at the close of the season… to be transferred to his most convenient bank. Also received $93.00 dues and receipts from movies which gave him a total of $767.09 in the treasury at the present time.

A $15.00 check was granted to the treasurer of the City County League for the forfeit money of the second team, which had to be posted at the March 2nd meeting. $5.00 bond was approved for treasurer's bond.

Author - Regarding the purchase of the ball diamond property… It was decided on a motion by Sidney Straley seconded by Carroll Hildebrand that we pay the $500.00 note which we've had for two years interest free of which $400.00 was to come out of the treasury and $100.00 which was received from the D.R.F. club. (**Author** – this is probably the note held by Nevin Smith, mentioned in the 1949 Narrative.)

The president appointed Nevin Smith, Sam Babble, and Carl Folkenroth as a committee to get the title to the ball field.

It was decided to purchase enough fertilizer and grass seed to feed the ballfield as necessary.

The second team will be in the City-County League. A Committee of Sam Babble, Nevin Smith, and Carl Folkenroth will arrange secure the Title for the Baseball field.

It was decided to get prices on new uniforms for the first team. Sporting Goods stores will be requested to have samples at the next meeting on March 13th. All players are required to bring their old uniforms. Measurements on players will be done at that meeting.

Approval was given to sponsor a Baseball for Boys Team, ages up to 15 years.

March 13, 1950

Special meeting was held in the C. L. Innerst's garage. President Herbert Geiselman presiding.

Old uniforms were brought back by most of the players from the first team from the year before as well as those on the second team which had come up to the first team.

Purchased uniforms included trousers, shirt, socks, and cap with lettering. Garments were washable and guaranteed not to shrink or fade for one year.

Author – For some photos of a typical uniform see the chapter "Building the Legacy". (Uniform shown owned by Gene Snyder).

After presentation on uniforms and discussion, it was decided to buy uniforms from Cohen Bros. at a cost of $19.00 each. Uniforms will be washable and guaranteed not to shrink or fade for one year. Bids had been received from Chet Patterson, Webb & Wolf, Cohen Bros. and Anderson Hardware.

March 28, 1950

Meeting was held in the C. L. Innerst's garage. President Herbert Geiselman presiding.

Treasurer reported receipts of $1313.11, expenses $1546.90, leaving $431.20 in the treasury.

Ralph Innerst was paid $10.00 for expenses incurred by use of his movie projector.

Progress was reported on the Score Card.

May Day festival to be held on May 16th, 1950.

Payment of $24.14 approved to P.A. & S. Small Co. for grass seed purchased.

Forfeit money was paid to the Southern York Co. League.

Author - Regarding the purchase of the ball diamond property…

The Jacobus Athletic Association approved the borrowing of $1,000.00 from Sam Babble to handle the debt as a first mortgage on property owned by Mont Smith that was bought in 1949 (by deed dated July 1st, 1949). The one (1) year mortgage cost will be 3%.

It was decided all members not paying dues by June 1st, 1950, shall be dismissed. On a motion by A. P. Falkenstine, seconded by Cletus Shive, it was decided to build a batting cage to help with batting practice. The first team will continue in the Southern York County League.

April 25, 1950

Meeting was held in the C. L. Innerst's garage. President Herbert Geiselman presiding.

The treasurer reported receipts of $198.00, expenses of $31.25, leaving a total of $511.99 in the treasury.

It was decided to pay Milt Baker for insurance - $170.00, Lawyer Rocco for searching title to the field etc. - $31.25 (**Author** - Regarding the purchase of the ball diamond property...), and pay the bill for the pipe for the batter's cage.

The May Day Festival will be held May 16th, rain date will be May 17th.

Nevin Smith was authorized to buy a mower for the field at "best price."

May 31, 1950

Meeting was held in the C. L. Innerst's garage. President Herbert Geiselman presiding.

Discussion was held on paying umpires $1.00 each to umpire Baseball for Boys games. It was also decided to buy baseballs for the Baseball for Boys, ages 13-15 team.

June 27, 1950

Meeting was held in the C. L. Innerst's garage. President Herbert Geiselman presiding.

The financial secretary reported $155.00 in the treasury.

Discussion was held regarding having a Carnival instead of a Picnic. It was decided to arrange a special "booster game" with Brogue for July 29th.

July 25, 1950

Meeting was held in the C. L. Innerst's garage. Vice President Norman Shearer presiding.

There was no treasurer's report for this month.

Discussion on having Carnival chances was held. Set-up for the Carnival will be needed. The Carnival will be held the beginning of August for four (4) days.

August 29, 1950

Meeting was held in the C. L. Innerst's garage. President Herbert Geiselman presiding.

A report on the Carnival was given by Mr. Babble with gross receipts for 4 nights being $3,239.78 plus raffle of $728.00 making a total of $3,967.78. Expenses at this time were not all figured yet.

New meeting night in the fire hall will be the third Wednesday of every month (from the last Tuesday of the month) in order to fit the fire hall schedule.

It was decided to meet at the Jacobus Fire Hall. Fee will be $ .50 per night. There was no final Carnival Finance Report at this meeting.

September 20, 1950

Meeting was held in the Jacobus Fire Hall. President Herbert Geiselman presiding.

From the Carnival... reported receipts $3270.93 and expenses of $2106.02. Raffle receipts were $728.00 with expenses of $211.85 leaving a net take of $1681.06 plus some inventory and a waffle iron!

In addition, first team gate receipts - $801.80, second team - $201.47, third team? - $51.99 making a total of $1055.26 for the year. Last year gate receipts for the first team alone were $2519.86.

It was decided to pay our loan and interest to Sam Babble, of $1,000.00 plus $7.50 interest. The Directors reported Amendments were made to the By-Laws, regarding the terms of the Directors. The terms will be three (3) years for two (2) people; two (2) years for one (1) person; and then two (2) people for one (1) year. After the third year all terms will be three (3) years.

It was decided to have an Athletic Association Banquet. Committee will be Bud Shearer, Nevin Smith and Red Arnold. It was also decided to have turkey for the dinner and be a mixed (spouses) gathering.

Everyone should turn in their uniforms from the past season to Paul Hildebrand. It was decided to buy two dozen baseball bats for next year.

November 22, 1950

Meeting was held in the Jacobus Fire Hall. President Herbert Geiselman presiding.

Banquet expenses reported as $196.50 and receipts from tickets sold as $138.20 making the net cost for the banquet $58.30. The treasurer's balance was reports as $952.00

The association voted to take over sponsorship of the basketball team, advancing them $22.50 for hall rentals for the past year.

It was reported Jake Myers would build a trophy case for team awards to be placed at the Jacobus Fire Hall.

(Author) – Once arrangements to meet with Linette Snyder of the Fire Company were made in 2016, the old trophies were eventually found in the basement of the current Fire Hall, covered in dust, and stuck in a pile on a shelf. Guess the trophy case was never constructed or if it was, it ended up being used for something else. Photos of the trophies are referenced in various places in the notes. As of now (7/8/2017), they remain in the fire hall basement. See Appendix D. for sample of photos taken from 7/8/2017.

The Association decided to sponsor the basketball team. The Banquet was declared a big success!

A D.R.F (Debt Retirement Fund) Club lottery was being conducted by the association, the proceeds of which can be used only to reduce the principal of our mortgage.

The treasurer reports a balance of $569.49 as of this date.

The Association decided to ask the Fire Company to allow basketball. A Committee of A. P. Falkenstine, Richard Bupp and Larry Smith will meet with the Fire Company regarding starting a basketball team to use the new Fire Hall.

New Officers elected for 1950 will be President, Herb Geiselman, Vice-President, Jesse Keeney, Treasurer, Curtis Darr, Recording Secretary, Carl Folkenroth, Financial Secretary, Sid Straley, Directors, Nevin Smith, Karl Smith, Clete Innerst, Howard Olp and A. P. Falkenstine.

Here is a copy of the Association's balance sheet at the end of 1950. Looks like there was around $961 in the Association treasury at this time.:

JACOBUS ATHLETIC ASSOCIATION INC.
Jacobus, Pa.

Auditor's Report
December 31, 1950

Receipts

Balance in Treas. 1-1-50.	$569.49
Membership Fees	2.00
Dues for 1950	135.00
Gate Receipts 1st. Team..	801.00
Gate Receipts 2nd. Team..	208.00
Gate Receipts Boy's Team.	51.99
Debt Retirement Fund	115.85
Punch Boards	105.97
Movies	65.29
Loan from S. C. Babble ..	1000.00
Score Card Adv.	532.00
Concessions	799.16
Insurance refunds	178.50
Carnival	3302.69
Raffle	776.38
Sale Athletic Equipment..	7.50
May Festival	56.95
Banquet	138.20
S.Y.C.L. Refund	20.83
City-County Refund	24.50
Boys Team Refund	10.00
TOTAL RECEIPTS 1950	8338.63
GRAND TOTAL	$ 8908.12

Administration	$ 46.80
Taxes	17.64
Equipment 1st Team	570.87
Equipment 2nd Team	242.08
Equipment Boys Team ...	39.93
Umpires 1st Team	222.00
Umpires 2nd Team	24.00
Player salaries & exp..	432.71
Forfeit money	55.00
Score cards	95.00
Concessions	496.19
Insurance-Player	175.00
Carnival	2097.72
Raffle	260.23
Medical	176.00
May Festival	38.69
Banquet	196.50
Nevin Smith pay. loan..	500.00
Mont Smith pay. mortg..	1000.00
S.C.Babble pay. mortg..	1000.00
Interest	30.00
Search & Record Deed...	31.25
Purchase power mower...	125.00
Basketball floor rent..	221.50
Miscellaneous-lawn seed batting cage, etc.	51.91
TOTAL EXPENSES 1950 ...	7947.02
Balance in Treasury December 31, 1950.	961.10
GRAND TOTAL	$ 8908.12

Audited by
C. Richard Bupp
Carl D. Arnold
Fred S. Shearer

January 25, 1951

Meeting was held in the Jacobus Fire Hall. President Herbert Geiselman presiding.

A report was given that the basketball team was achieving some success with a .500 or better average. They have acquired uniforms. Motion was made for the Association to pay hall rent and expenses.

The Election Committee Chairman, Jesse Keeney reported the Directors for three (3) years will be Clete Innerst and A. P. Falkenstine. The two (2) year Director will be Nevin Smith, and the one (1) year Director will be Howard Olp and Karl Smith. The Officers elected Red Arnold, President; Norman Shearer, Vice-President; Carl Folkenroth, Financial Secretary; Rich Arnold, Recording Secretary; Curtis Darr, Treasurer.

It was decided the Carnival this year will be 50/50 with the Jacobus Fire Company. Richard Bupp, Fred Shearer and Red Arnold were designated for the Audit Committee.

Richard Bupp reported the basketball team was winning about 50% of their games. They have also bought uniforms for the team. Elmer Geiselman moved, seconded by Karl Smith that the Association will pay $23.50 for some of the rentals at Seven Valleys Fire Hall.

February 17, 1951

Meeting was held in the Jacobus Fire Hall. President Carl Arnold presiding.

It was reported that 2 dozen bats had arrived with a motion that 2 dozen more be ordered.

Carl Folkenroth was appointed Business Manager; Norman Shearer will represent the first team, and Richard Bupp will represent the second team. It was decided to buy twelve (12) uniforms for the second team. Cohen Bros. will make arrangements to do measurements in March. Repairs will be made to the backstop and batting cage.

Grover Kirschner and Jerry Darr were accepted as new members.

March 21, 1951

Meeting was held in the Jacobus Fire Hall. President Carl Arnold presiding.

The basketball team was reported as improving.

Motion made to pay standing bills to Webb & Wolf, Karl Folkenroth, Clete Innerst, and the firehall rent.

Added three (3) more second team uniforms, total will now be fifteen (15) to the order. The Baseball for Boys program will use V.F.W. rules so the team can compete in local tournaments. Grover Kirschner was selected to manage the first team in the Southern York County League. Indications are looking like the City-County League will be ready for the second team.

It was decided May Day will be on May 10th.

April 18, 1951

Meeting was held in the Jacobus Fire Hall. President Carl Arnold presiding.

There was a discussion about Sunday baseball played at home. It was agreed that more work is to be done on the infield – to contact Pally Innerst for this.

Bills paid to Anstadt Printing, Seven Valleys fire hall rent, Baseball for Boys, and Rich Arnold.

Carroll Hildebrand will be Baseball for Boys Manager as Richard Bupp reported he was going into the Armed Forces. Red Arnold, President, will be City-County League Representative. Ted Arnold will be considered a new Junior member. Cletus Shive was appointed grounds keeper.

May 16, 1951

Meeting was held in the Jacobus Fire Hall. President Carl Arnold presiding.

Bills paid to Cohen's, G.F.T.Pl.H (**Author** – I have no idea what this is)., Webb & Wolf, Stallmans, and Smalls.

Baseball bats and other supplies were approved for all three teams.

June 20, 1951

Meeting was held in the Jacobus Fire Hall. President Carl Arnold presiding.

It was voted to pay Roy Warfel $3.00 per game for six (6) games as a pitcher.

July 25, 1951

Meeting was held in the Jacobus Fire Hall. President Carl Arnold presiding.

It was decided to purchase a new first base mitt.

Elwood Chronister, a new player, will receive expense money to get to ball games. (**Author** – my Dad has no idea what this was about)

September 19, 1951

Meeting was held in the Jacobus Fire Hall. President Carl Arnold presiding.

Reports were received from all three (3) baseball teams. It was decided to have a Banquet again, and it will be held at the Jacobus Fire Hall. LeRoy Myers paid $4.00 for (45) cement blocks that were left over from bleacher construction. No response from Jacobus Fire Company on basketball in Fire Hall. Following discussion, basketball will stay at Seven Valleys.

October, 1951

No meeting. Banquet was held. Good attendance.

November 28, 1951

Meeting was held in the Jacobus Fire Hall. President Carl Arnold presiding.

Basketball committee was appointed – Norman Shearer, Jake Meyers, Rich Arnold, and Gerry Snyder. The directors plan to meet with the Fire Co. officials for reconsideration of use of the hall for basketball.

Thanks to Dr. Getz for donating his time for the football team, and also the insurance refunds he returned to the Association.

December 26, 1951

Meeting was held in the Jacobus Fire Hall. President Carl Arnold presiding.

Report that $1624.70 was the balance in the treasury.

Basketball floor available every Friday night and Sunday afternoon for $5.00.

Decision was made to buy a $1,000.00 Savings Bond from the Treasurer's Fund. Norman Shearer reported the Fire Hall floor was ready for basketball.

The Officers elected for 1952 were: President, Red Arnold; Vice President, Bud Shearer; Financial Secretary, Carl Folkenroth; Recording Secretary, Clarke Shearer; Treasurer, Curtis Darr; Director's for three (3) years: William Darr and Howard Olp. For two (2) years, A. P. Falkenstine and Clete Innerst. One (1) year, Grover Kirschner. It was decided to pay the Fire Company an $8.00 rental fee for 1952 (**Author** – for Association Meetings, I think).

January 16, 1952

Meeting was held in the Jacobus Fire Hall.

Decided to sponsor three (3) baseball teams again in the same leagues. Basketball was reported to be going good. We paid three (3) weeks rent of $15.00 to Seven Valleys Fire Company. Red Arnold appointed a Carnival Committee that included all officers and directors plus Rich Arnold, Pret Hershner, Ervin Myers, Nevin Smith, Fred Shearer, Pete Shearer, Gene Snyder, Sid Straley and Bob Falkenstine.

February 20, 1952

Meeting was held in the Jacobus Fire Hall.

No openings were available in the Twilight League this year, according to a letter from the league secretary.

A new By-laws amendment was introduced – (**Author** - All persons could apply for membership, dues would be $1 per year paid by April 30th, and members would be notified of unpaid dues before being dropped as members.)

So far only four teams were represented in the City County League this year.

Motion was withdrawn on purchasing $1000 G Series bond because it did not pay any interest. Instead a motion was made to purchase a $1000 CD for 6 months.

Balance in the treasury - $1577.69.

Meeting was held in the Fire Hall. A review of the new amendment that was developed was made. No changes occurred. Will be voted on at the March meeting. We paid $30.00 basketball rent and $1.50 for a new score book. It was decided to put $1,000.00 on a Certificate of Deposit. New members added were Glenn Shive, son of Cletus Shive and Dennis and Robert McWilliams, sons of Palmer McWilliams.

March 19, 1952

Meeting was held in the Jacobus Fire Hall.

New amendment about membership rules was approved (Article 3).

Meeting was called by Grover Kershner for March 23 in the Fire Hall for all prospective ballplayers.

Bills were paid: postage - $4.94, Hall rent for basketball - $25.00, Treasurer's Bond - $5.00, Bruce V. Smith - $1.97, and forfeit money for the Southern Your County League - $40.00.

Decided to get two (2) load of topsoil. Added a backstop for the visitors' bullpen. Paid $40.00 to the Southern York County League for our forfeit money.

April 16, 1952

Meeting was held in the Jacobus Fire Hall.

Bills were $124.80 for bats and $36.00 to P.A. and S. Small.

The next Southern York County meeting to be held in Shrewsbury on April 30th.

An inquiry was made on insurance for baseball, basketball and football. Because of high cost, it was decided to only continue insurance for baseball. It was reported we need to track down two (2) catcher's mitts, owned by the association that are missing.

May 21, 1952

Meeting was held in the Jacobus Fire Hall.

Motion to pay all bills totaling $287.37.

Received rosters of all Southern York County League teams. Paid bills totaling $287.37. (President, Red Arnold was absent. He was married Saturday, May 17th. He was travelling across New York State to Niagara Falls.)

(**Author** – no **June** meeting notes)

July 16, 1952

Meeting was held in the Jacobus Fire Hall.

Agreed to bills to be paid.

It was reported at the Southern League meeting, that discussion was held regarding umpires.

(**Author** – no **August** meeting notes)

September 17, 1952

Meeting was held in the Jacobus Fire Hall.

(Note from Author - Not positive what the deal was with the chicken houses but in a few more meetings it appears that they were looking into a building for concessions and equipment storage.)

Received $10.00 of our Baseball for Boys forfeit fund. Decided to again sponsor a basketball team. Paid a bill received from the grounds keeper. A. P. Falkenstine was appointed to contact Harry Boyer regarding chicken houses he had for sale. (**Author** - Harry Boyer is an elementary school teacher and lives on a farm south of Bob Wiley's Restaurant, a little south of Jacobus)

(**Author** – no **October** meeting notes)

November 19, 1952

Meeting was held in the Jacobus Fire Hall.

Cars were reported to be going on the ballfield, racing, and tearing it up, thus the items listed in the paragraph below were discussed.

Harry Boyer decided he was not going to sell the chicken houses. Clair Smith will check on costs for a 12' x 14' building for concession and equipment storage use. It will be made of cinder block or cement blocks.

It was decided to buy a 385' piece of land from Mont Smith. Cost to be not more than $6.00 per foot. (**Author** – this is the property across Pleasant Avenue from the ball diamond where the basketball court, tennis court, and other facilities are now located.)

Received $24.60 from the Southern York County League. A carnival check equal to $1,105.72 was received. Richard Bupp/Bob Falkenstine were appointed as business managers for the basketball team.

In order to keep cars off of the baseball field, it was decided to purchase either chain or cable, whatever the best price would be. Also, we will get signs posted about property damage. Nominations for officers were made. No names were listed in the minutes.

December 17, 1952

Meeting was held in the Jacobus Fire Hall.

Two outstanding bills were paid.

Received a postal money order for $10.00 as a donation from Harry McLaughlin. (The McLaughlin's lived on a farm north of Jacobus along the Codorus Creek.)

The land extension purchase has been agreed to with Mont and Anna Mary Smith. The transaction will be completed in the spring of 1953. In the minutes it is described as "the land opposite to the ball diamond". (**Author** – this is the property across Pleasant Avenue from the ball diamond where the basketball court, tennis court, and other facilities are now located.)

It was decided to table the concession stand building for the present time.

Chains were purchased to put around the ball field.

It was decided to use Clete Innerst's garage again for meetings.

Officers for 1953 will be: Norman Shearer, President; Red Arnold, Vice President; Financial Secretary, Carl Folkenroth; Recording Secretary, Clarke Shearer; Treasurer, Jesse Keeney; Director for three (3) years was Grover Kirschner. The appointed Auditing Committee will be Carroll Hildebrand, Bob Falkenstine and Fred Shearer.

January 21, 1953

Meeting was held in the Jacobus Fire Hall.

Instead of chain for along the streets, it was decided to use ½" dia. cable to be donated by Clete Innerst.

Discussion was again held about the meeting place. It was decided to continue meeting back in the fire hall.

The Score Card Committee for the year will be: Carroll Hildebrand, Jesse Keeney, Lee Arnold, Karl Smith and Red Arnold.

Carnival Committee for the year will be: Norman Shearer, Red Arnold, Jesse Keeney, Clarke Shearer, William Darr, Howard Olp, Grover Kirschner, Lee Arnold, Pete Shearer, Karl Smith, Fred S. Shearer, Ralph Innerst, Curtis Darr, Sid Straley, Nevin

Smith, Gene Snyder, Bill Shearer, Danny Smith, Ron Bohnert, Fred C. Shearer, Russ Shearer and Curt Bohnert.

March 18, 1953

Meeting was held in the Jacobus Fire Hall.

It was announced that the application was accepted for a berth in the Central York Co. League. The Goldsmith ball was adopted and the services of the York Co. Umpires Assoc. contracted for.

It was suggested that a number of bids be asked for on the building to be built behind the backstop.

Carroll Hildebrand accepted the post of Business Manager for the year.

Norman Shearer was elected manager of the baseball team in the Central York Co. League.

Arthur Shearer was directed to by the pipe and fittings needed to run the water up to the ball diamond.

April 15, 1953

Meeting was held in the Jacobus Fire Hall.

The scorecard committee reported very good progress filling the ads. (**Author** - See the sample scorecard in the chapter on "The Money Game").

After no other bids were given, Clair Smith was instructed to go ahead and start building the concessions/storage building. At this time, it was ready for the roof.

Jake Myers is going to put some cupboards in the building as soon as it is completed.

Jesse Keeney volunteered to help Cletus Shive to take care of the grounds.

Jesse Keeney was to get the plumbers to get connected into the main water line. Ralph Innerst will dig the ditch.

June 24, 1953

Meeting was held in the Jacobus Fire Hall.

Just a few advertisements remaining on the score card.

The president reported that the businessmen of the town have donated money to buy uniforms for the baseball for boys' team.

Curtis Bohnert has been appointed grounds keeper in place of Cletus Shive.

A letter of thanks was read from the Jacobus Mother's Club expressing thanks for use of the facilities for their May Day Fete.

It was agreed that the assoc. will put a down payment on the field, whatever was available, and Mont Smith will hold the deed until we pay the remainder. (Author** – this is the property across Pleasant Avenue from the ball diamond where the basketball court, tennis court, and other facilities are now located.)

July 15, 1953

Meeting was held in the Jacobus Fire Hall.

Motion was made that the assoc. pay $1150.00 for the ground purchased from Mont Smith – this amount being half of the price. Motion was carried. (Author** – this is the property across Pleasant Avenue from the ball diamond where the basketball court, tennis court, and other facilities are now located.)

There was a discussion on what would be done with the ground being bought. Nothing was decided at this time.

September 16, 1953

Meeting was held in the Jacobus Fire Hall.

Carl Folkenroth reported $1200.00 was paid on the land we bought from Mont Smith. We still owe $979.00 on this debt.

Carrol Hildebrand, Ervin Myers, Jesse Keeney, Earl Hildebrand, and Grover Kirchner were appointed for the laying out of temporary plans for the playground to be started and also to contact other organizations about joining us in this venture.

A motion was made that Earl Hildebrand take the Baseball for Boys team out for a meal, then turn the bill into the Association. (**Author** – the BFB team was 1953 champs – see the photos of the trophy in the appendix D.)

The treasurer reported a balance of $172.67 as of this date.

November 18, 1953

Meeting was held in the Jacobus Fire Hall.

Arthur Shearer made a motion, seconded by A. P. Falkenstine, that we pay off the land we bought from Mont Smith, this year yet. Motion carried.

December 23, 1953

Meeting was held in the Jacobus Fire Hall.

The President reported that Carl Folkenroth has the check ready to pay the field in full just as soon as Mont Smith comes back from Florida.

Mention was made that repairs had to be done to the backstop and other fences in front of the bleachers.

Officers elected for next year:

President – Russel Shearer
Vice-President – Carl D. Arnold
Financial Secretary – Carl Folkenroth
Assistant Financial Secretary – Erwin Shearer
Recording Secretary – Clark V. Shearer
Assistant Recording Secretary – Lee Arnold
Treasurer – Richard Bupp
Assistant Treasurer – Curtis Darr
3 yr. Directors – Ervin Myers, Jesse Keeney
2 yr. Directors – Grover Kirchner
1 yr. Directors – William Darr, Howard Olp
Auditing committee – William Klein, Fred S. Shearer, Ronald Bohnert

January 27, 1954

Meeting was held in the Jacobus Fire Hall.

A big town-wide membership drive is to be started. West of the Trail – Lee Arnold and Stephen Hershner and Perry Innerst; North on the Trail – Ronald and Curtis Bohnert and Perry Innerst; South on the Trail – Carl D. Arnold, William

Shearer, and Gene Snyder; East of the Trail – Jesse Keeney and Arthur Shearer.

There was a discussion about securing some kind of "old rig" that will run, for the use of the ground keeper on the diamond. (**Author** – Looking at future entries in the minutes, "old rig" appears to be something to mow with and do ground maintenance with.)

Carroll Hildebrand would accept the post of Business Manager for the year 1954.

Motion was made to retain the berth in the Central York Co. League for the 1954 season.

A motion was made that two 21 ft. length of pipes be purchased. (**Author** – For what, the minutes don't say at this point.)

February 17, 1954

Meeting was held in the Jacobus Fire Hall.

The playground committee reported that they have rough plans for the playground.

The Central York Baseball League team opens at Emigsville on Saturday May 1.

Insurance was purchased once again for the baseball teams.

Curtis Darr was appointed to make some signs concerning our not being responsible for accidents.

Members appointed to the playground committee: Carroll Hildebrand, Ervin Meyers, Jesse Keeney, Earl Hildebrand, and Grover Kirchner.

The membership campaign netted 80 new members to date.

Clair Smith made a motion for a committee be appointed to make arrangements for a collection through the town for money to be used exclusively for playground equipment. The playground committee will take care of this.

Norman Shearer will be the manager of the Central York League Team for 1954.

Appointed to the carnival committee for this year; Russell Shearer, Carl D. Arnold, Clarke Shearer, Richard Bupp, Ervin Meyers, Norman Shearer, Jesse Keeney, W. G. Darr, Howard Olp, Grover Kirchner, Lee Arnold, Arthur Shearer, Karl Smith, Fred S. Shearer, Fred C. Shearer, Curtis Darr, Sid Straley, Nevin Smith, William Shearer, Donald Smith, Ronald Bohnert, Curtis Bohnert, Roger Arnold, Stephen Kershner, Raymond Smith, Ervin Shearer, Herbert Geiselman.

March 17, 1954

Meeting was held in the Jacobus Fire Hall.

Carroll Hildebrand reported that 200 lbs. of grass seed had been purchased for the playground.

It was reported that the Central League ok'd the rosters and schedule for the upcoming year. They also favored setting up a baseball commissioner for York Co.

Concession committee appointed – Fred C. Shearer, Wm. G. Darr, and Clarke V. Shearer

Ticket committee appointed – A.P. Falkenstein, Howard Olp, Grover Kirchner, Raymond Smith, and Richard Bupp.

April 21, 1954

Meeting was held in the Jacobus Fire Hall, president Russell Shearer presiding.

Playground is being plowed, leveled, and grass seed planted.

There was a discussion as to when the shed can be put up for the storage of the mowers and the car which was purchased by the Association. This car is a 1935 Chevrolet that was bought for $10.00.

The scoreboard is to be moved onto the front of the shed as soon as the shed is completed… in center field, back of the flag pole.

May 19, 1954

Meeting was held in the Jacobus Fire Hall, president Russell Shearer presiding.

Warm up pitching rubbers and back-stops have been put up and complete.

The title for the automobile purchased was received. It was decided to return the title to the original owner and let him send the title to Harrisburg as junk. (**Author** – Not sure what went on here with the auto.)

It was decided that Jesse Keeney, Steve Hershner, and Daniel Smith will take charge of an organized program for the baseball for boys' team on Tuesday and Thursday afternoons, with the express purpose of helping the kids learn more about baseball.

July 21, 1954

Meeting was held in the Jacobus Fire Hall, president Russell Shearer presiding.

Central League All-Star game will be played August 8th. The players from Jacobus are Russel Shearer, Lee Arnold, Ronald Bohnert, and Dale Innerst.

A motion was made to pay the Real Estate Transfer tax to have the deed recorded. This tax amounted to 1% of the buying price, which is about $22.00.

A motion was made to give $50.00 to the Fire Company to help defray expenses concurred during the carnival week.

A good deal of discussion as to having a second team next year to make a place for some of the younger players. Discussion was postponed until next spring. (**Author** – Not sure what this point was about. Up to this point I hadn't noticed that the second team was not in operation. Looking back, it appears that the last mention of a second team was back in November 1952.)

September 15, 1954

Meeting was held in the Jacobus Fire Hall, president Russell Shearer presiding.

The mowers are to be sharpened in the coming week and the man sharpening them said we should have something to pull the mowers slower to keep from knocking them apart. Along this line, it was decided to sell the Chevrolet for as much as we can get for it. (**Author** – it appears now that the 1935 Chevrolet was being used to tow the mowers!)

Richard Geiselman made a motion that we buy a tractor with or without a cycle bar for approximately $150.00 to be bought by a committee appointed by the President. The committee was – Russell Shearer, Richard Bupp, Russel Lentz, Jesse Keeny and Earl Hildebrand.

Richard Bupp reported our share of the carnival was $725.85 minus the $50.00 voted to give to the Fire Hall for use of the building. The total take was $675.85.

It was mentioned that a score card should be sold next year and to get it started early in the spring.

December 20, 1954

Meeting was held in the Jacobus Fire Hall, president Russell Shearer presiding.

The tractor committee reported progress and that they are still looking around.

It was decided to accept the offer of a building from Paul Hildebrand. All we had to do is move it.

The following officers were elected to the 1955 year:

President – Lee Arnold

Vice President – Carroll Hildebrand

Financial Secretary – Carl Folkenroth

Recording Secretary – Clarke V. Shearer

Treasurer – Richard Bupp

Director – William G. Darr and Raymond Smith – for three years

Auditing Committee – Norman Shearer, Ronald Bohnert, and Robert Klinedinst

A motion was made to pay the $6.00 Fire Hall rent for the year 1954.

January 19, 1955

Meeting was held in the Jacobus Fire Hall, president Lee Arnold presiding.

There was a good deal of discussion as to the coming year for baseball. It was decided to send a representative to the Susquehanna League meeting to see what their set up is.

The scorecard committee for the season – Jesse Keeney, Richard Arnold, Raymond Smith, Steven Hershner, Carroll Hildebrand, and Carl Folkenroth.

It was agreed to pay to water bill.

February 21, 1955

Meeting was held in the Jacobus Fire Hall, president Lee Arnold presiding.

The scorecard committee reported progress with some new advertisers and most of the spaces being sold.

A motion was made to have the transmission (**Author**: Of the mower?) torn out and repaired for a cost of not more than $25.

It was reported that the Susquehanna league would not accept our application because of the policy of the league not wanting teams from towns of more than one team. (**Author** – Is there still a second team in town at this point? Haven't heard anything about it for a while.)

Forfeit money of $17.92 for the Central League would be due on March 11.

A letter was received from Sterling Ecker about the Baseball for Boys program concerning the county having their own program… excluding the city all together. A motion was made that our organization go along with this program

The Central League now has a 35-game schedule, lengthening the season. The idea being to play the extra games in twilight.

A load of top soil for the infield will be purchased from Ralph Innerst for $32.00.

The president appointed the carnival committee for the year.

Membership committee appointments:
Seven Valleys Rd. and Pleasant Avenue – Carl D. Arnold
Main St. – Bruce Smith
North – Russell Shearer, Robert Olp, and Earl Hildebrand
Church St. and Water St. – Norman Shearer, Clarke V. Shearer, Carroll Hildebrand, and Herry Lee Darr
South – Richard Bupp, Grover Kirchner, and Arthur Shearer.

Preston Hershner and William Heltzel were nominated for manager of the Central League Team. Preston Hershner was elected.

March 21, 1955

Meeting was held in the Jacobus Fire Hall, vice president Carroll Hildebrand presiding.

A letter was received from Sterling Ecker asking to hold a meeting here in Jacobus for the purpose of organizing the Baseball for Boys program for this season.

Motion made to burn the grass on the playground at the earliest possible time. (**Author**– What? To get ready to re-seed again maybe?)

Carroll Hildebrand and Norman Shearer were appointed business managers (**Author** – of the Central League team?)

There was a discussion about what kind of equipment to put up in the playground – homemade or custom built.

Motion was made to buy insurance for the First Team and the Baseball for Boys teams.

The Scorecard was reported ready with only one $10 ad remaining to be sold.

Motion was made to give the May Day ribbon to the PTA of the school (**Author** – Not sure what the May Day ribbon was.)

Plitts soda got an exclusive right to sell soda at the ball diamond for this summer.

It was approved to put a $100 check into the carnival fund for this year.

A motion to rent a Safe Deposit box for the Associations important papers was approved.

April 20, 1955

Meeting was held in the Jacobus Fire Hall, president Lee Arnold presiding.

The scorecard committee reported that the scorecard was at the printers and most of the money was in for the ads

A motion was made and approved to buy 125 ft. of garden hose.

A motion was made and approved to buy a First Aid kit.

A motion was made and approved to pay all bills.

May 25, 1955

Meeting was held in the Jacobus Fire Hall, president Lee Arnold presiding.

It was reported that the swings have been started on the playground. With seats of all kinds ordered, playground links for chains. After the Holidays should be able to cement the swings in.

First aid kits have been purchased, one for each team. Some hose has also been purchased. Cletus Innerst to put some cinders on the road back of the backstop. After that some roofing tabs will be put on the road to the end of the bleachers.

Jesse Keeney and Earl Hildebrand would appreciate any help that anybody can give them during their practice sessions or when they play. ...just to help them teach the boys more about baseball.

A motion was made that we offer $2 to the men who will go along with the second team, to umpire for them.

A motion was made to pay all the current bills.

September 28, 1955

Meeting was held in the Jacobus Fire Hall, president Lee Arnold presiding.

A new pole has been obtained for the one end of the back-stop and will be put in place on Saturday morning, along with some other boards that need replacing.

There was some discussion as to the possibility of backing a basketball team this winter. Nothing was decided.

A motion was made to pay all the current bills.

January 18, 1956

Meeting was held in the Jacobus Fire Hall, president Lee Arnold presiding.

The results of the election for 1956:

President – Lee Arnold
Vice President – Earl Hildebrand
Financial Secretary – Carl D. Arnold
Recording Secretary – Robert Falkenstine
Assistant Secretary – Steve Hershner
Treasurer – Carl Folkenroth
Director – Bud Shearer
Auditors – Fred Shearer and Bud Shearer

It was decided that we enter teams in the Central, Amateur, and Baseball for Boys leagues.

It was also decided to go in with Fire Company on the Carnival again this year.

March 4, 1956

Meeting was held in the Jacobus Fire Hall, president Lee Arnold presiding.

Auditors report showed a balance of $911.63.

Bills paid included $13.28 forfeit money for the Central League and $100 for the Carnival.

New business included election of the ball team field managers

Norman Shearer – manager of the Central League team
Carl D. Arnold – manager of the Amateur League team
Baseball for Boys managers delayed to a later time.

It was moved and seconded that trophies be purchased for the baseball for boy's teams and try to secure uniforms for the 13 to 15 age group through the towns businessmen. All the teams will be furnished caps.

Carrol Hildebrand will be contacted to serve as business manager.

March 23, 1956

Meeting was held in the Jacobus Fire Hall, vice president Carroll Hildebrand presiding.

The meeting opened with a briefing by Clair Trout on the playground set up. The securing of a playground director is to be done by contacting our school board. The state will pay 75% of his salary while we the association will pay 25%. A director gets an average of $50 a week for a usual 10-week period. If a certified phys. Ed. Teacher cannot be secured as a director there is a possibility of getting an emergency certificate for another capable person.

It was moved and seconded that Richard Bupp contact the school board in regards to securing a playground director for this summer.

It was decided to have quarry waste put on the road at the ball diamond. It was also decided to retain insurance for the teams, going into effect April 1st.

Received 5 bags of free fertilizer for the ball field from Koller Fertilizer Co. through William Hildebrand.

Carroll Hildebrand has been secured as business manager for the ball team.

April 18, 1956

Meeting was held in the Jacobus Fire Hall, president Lee Arnold presiding.

It was pointed out that in order to go through with the securing of a director we the association would have to put up $400 because the school board does not have the funds and the state is slow in appropriating such funds… so it was moved and seconded that we pay only the 25% and no more… which means that we will probably not get a director this year.

It was moved and seconded that the quarry waste not be used and that oil be put on instead.

It was decided to pay bills who total amount was $183.

Ground Rules were revamped a little.

October 3, 1956

Meeting was held in the Jacobus Fire Hall, president Lee Arnold presiding.

There was a lay-off in having meetings due to the summer's busy schedule…

The worth of a playground director was debated including the number of boys that were profiting from this program. (**Author** – since there were no additional notes recorded since April, I'm not sure what all went on and if a playground director *was* eventually hired for the summer, there is no information about it recorded.)

It was moved and seconded that the old dug-outs and backstop be torn down and new ones erected. It was decided to work on this project every Saturday after the World Series is over. All men are urged to be there.

All bills were to be paid.

February 13, 1957

Meeting was held in the Jacobus Fire Hall.

The results of the election for 1957:

President – Gene Snyder
Vice President – Earl Hildebrand
Financial Secretary – Carl D. Arnold
Recording Secretary – Robert Falkenstine
Treasurer – Carl Folkenroth
Directors – Lee Arnold and Mervin Slenker, Jr.
Auditors – Fred Shearer and Bud Shearer

There was some discussion about the Jacobus Recreation Association being able to erect a building on the Athletic Association property. Carl D. Arnold will look into the legal end of the matter.

March 22, 1957

Meeting was held in the Jacobus Fire Hall.

The request by the about the Jacobus Recreation Association being able to erect a building on the Athletic Association property was rejected.

Jesse Keeney was elected the manager for the Central League team.

Carl D. Arnold declined the manager position for the second team. It was decided to let that ride until the next meeting.

Work on the diamond was to take place in the evening this coming week with as many to be there as often as possible.

January 29, 1958

Meeting was held in the Jacobus Fire Hall.

Auditing committee appointed – Carl D. Arnold, Carl Folkenroth, and Jay Snyder

Gene Snyder is looking into a playground director.

Motion made to enter teams in the four leagues we were in last year. (**Author** – Guessing these to be Central League, Amateur League, Baseball for Boys 8 – 12, and Baseball for Boys 13 – 15?)

Motion made to go in on the Carnival again this year.

There was a discussion about putting a roof over the bleachers.

Nominations for Officers for 1958:

President – Gene Snyder, Jesse Keeney, Richard Arnold
Treasurer – Carl Folkenorth
Financial Secretary – Bob Arnold
Secretary – Jay Snyder, Ronnie Bohnert, George Arnold
Directors – Fred S. Shearer, William G. Darr, Gerry Snyder, Raymond Smith, Jerry Lee Darr

March 23, 1958

Meeting was held in the Jacobus Fire Hall. Gene Snyder presiding.

Last year's accident insurance claims were discussed.

Regarding a playground director, it was decided to contact a number of people to see who can be obtained for the job.

Elected officers for 1958:

President – Gene Snyder
Vice President – Jesse Keeney
Secretary – Jay Snyder
Assistant Secretary - George Arnold
Financial Secretary – Bob Arnold
Treasurer – Carl Folkenroth
Director – Fred D. Shearer and Jerry Darr

It was decided to contact Les Williams to see if he was available to manage for the upcoming year.

Work on the diamond would take place on the next Saturday.

It was decided to buy nine pair of pants, 15 pair of stockings, and caps for the first team.

It was decided to sell the old car as junk.

It was motioned that insurance be fully covered for all four teams. An individual player has to make sure his claim is filled out by the doctor.

The meeting was adjourned and a film of the All Star game was shown.

June 18, 1958

Meeting was held in the Jacobus Fire Hall. Gene Snyder presiding.

Discussion was held on giving the Church a right of way for a road in the right field of the ball diamond. Motion was made to give the right of way. The Association officers will serve as the committee to meet with the building committee of the Reformed Church. (**Author** – this is a little confusing as the UCC church was eventually built across the street from center field. Maybe this road was for construction reasons?)

$10 was given to Gerry Snyder for a hot plate.

A check for $100 was written for a deposit toward the carnival.

February 1, 1959

Meeting was held in the Jacobus Fire Hall.

Officers elected for 1959:

President: Fritz Shearer
Vice President: Jay Snyder
Recording Secretary: Barry Shearer
Assistant Secretary: George Arnold
Director: Bud Shearer

Motion was made and seconded to have a team in the Central League.

Lee Arnold, Mervin Slenker, and Jay Snyder were nominated to a committee to find a new tractor.

Still looking into the possibility of putting a roof on the bleachers.

March 15, 1959

Meeting was held in the Jacobus Fire Hall.

A report will be given at the next meeting on the price of purchasing a tractor.

All officers were appointed to serve on the Carnival committee.

A manager for the season will be selected at the next meeting.

A discussion was held on the possibility of hiring a playground director.

The motion was carried to have schedule cards made up again for the coming season. The committee appointed for this task was Gerry Snyder, Mervin Slenker, Bob Arnold, and Carl Folkenroth.

April 5, 1959

Meeting was held in the Jacobus Fire Hall.

Discussion of buying a tractor was continued. It was decided that nothing less than 5 H. P. be purchased. The sale of the current gang mowers was also discussed but no further action was taken.

Getting a playground director was still a problem. If no one else can be obtained someone from town may be asked to take over both Baseball for Boys teams.

Each block on the new scorecards will be sold for $5.00.

A motion was made and seconded that caps be kept the same color as last year.

A motion was made by Jay Snyder, seconded by Lee Arnold, that the Jacobus Borough Council take over ownership of the ball diamond and the playground. The idea of this being the borough could then lease it back to the Association and also protect it from being sold. A committee of officers and directors are to attend the next borough council meeting.

Russ Shearer was elected as manager for the first team.

John Grove showed a variety of jackets of which to choose from. The Jackets acknowledge that fact of winning the Amateur League Championship (**Author** – 1958 Champs.). They can come with or without emblems.

May 3, 1959

Meeting was held in the Jacobus Fire Hall.

A tractor was purchased from Innerst's.

Motion was made and approved to get Barry Stein for playground director. Later is was found out that Stein was not available.

It was decided to have a work night to fix the small diamond for play. (**Editor** – not sure what/where the "small diamond" is.)

It was decided to have a team in the Amateur League. Carl Folkenroth will serve as manager.

The directors and officers are to attend the next borough council meeting for the purpose of setting the borough to take over the diamond and playground.

There was a discussion of Donkey Baseball. It was decided that we check with the Lions Club before taking action.

It was discovered by the Treasurer that we have to file an income tax report to the government from 1947 to the present. The Treasurers bond and players insurance were paid.

The gang mower is to be fixed up and then advertised for sale.

June 5, 1959

Meeting was held in the Jacobus Fire Hall.

It was voted that Larry Shearer take charge of our playground for the summer. It was brought up that equipment for him would have to be provided.

Progress was reported on the schedule cards.

At the next meeting, the association is to sign the property to the borough if the deed suits. (**Author** – see the Final Deed documents from 1959 in Appendix A.)

Gang mowers were fixed and are still to be painted before being advertised.

It was decided that the Lions Club was to take care of the Donkey Baseball game this year.

Motion was approved to cement under the building moved from town. Jake Myers was suggested to do it.

January 31, 1960

Meeting was held in the Jacobus Fire Hall.

Discussion about what to do about an old tractor. It was decided to get Heine Heltzel to come and get it for junk.

It was also decided to fix the gang mowers to sell and see about getting the new building cemented.

A committee was appointed to reorganize the score cards and to sell the remaining ads. The committee was – Lee Arnold, Jerry Darr, Carl Folkenroth, and Merv Slenker.

Officers elected for 1960:

President: Merv Slenker
Vice President: George Arnold
Financial Secretary: Ted Arnold
Recording Secretary: Barry Shearer
Assistant Secretary: Jay Snyder
Treasurer: Carl Folkenroth
Directors: Fred C. Shearer and Lee Arnold

March 27, 1960

Meeting was held in the Jacobus Fire Hall.

A motion was approved to have a playground director. It was decided to try and get Larry Shearer again.

Discussions about painting the bleachers and tearing down the score desk. (**Author** – Not sure what the "score desk" was.)

Discussion about getting materials for the backstop on the small diamond. Nothing definite was decided. (**Author** – Not positive, but I recall a diamond at the far end of center field of the main diamond. Maybe this was what is referred to as the "small diamond". There were some hand-written notes stuck in the minutes about this being the Baseball for Boys diamond.)

A committee was appointed to look for a manager for the season. Committee was – Gene Snyder, Lee Arnold, and Jay Snyder.

It was approved to give a $100 check to the carnival committee.

May 1, 1960

Meeting was held in the Jacobus Fire Hall.

It was again decided to get Larry Shearer for Playground director. It was decided to tear down the score desk but not paint the bleachers (**Author** – Again, not sure what the "score desk" was.)

It was noted that 5 truckloads of ground would be needed for the infield.

The manager of the Central League team this year will be William Heltzel. At this point the Amateur League team manager was not known.

The borough would be getting the materials for the Baseball for Boys back stop and the association would be putting it up.

The cost for the fence in right field was to be split between the ball club and the man at Orwig's. (**Author** – not sure who "Orwig's was. I assume he lived in the house in right field.) It was also brought up that Bob Franklin said he would contribute $50 to the ball club because of the construction of his swimming pool interfering with the upkeep of the diamond.

No future meetings were planned at this time.

March 19, 1961

Meeting was held in the Jacobus Fire Hall.

Officers elected for 1961:

President – George Arnold
Vice President – Barry Shearer
Financial Secretary – Ted Arnold

Recording Secretary – Mark Innerst
Treasurer – Carl Folkenroth
Directors – Gene Snyder and Jerry Darr

It was decided to pay $1 to the borough for the use of the diamond.

It was decided to get Larry Shearer for playground director and if was not available, to possibly get Barry Shearer.

It was announced that there would be two Baseball for Boys teams.

All were to report for a work day on the next Saturday.

Bud Shearer was to check with Bob Franklin on the $50 he promised to pay due to the interference with diamond maintenance cause by his pool construction.

A committee would be looking into possible managers for the Central League Team.

April 9, 1961

Meeting was held in the Jacobus Fire Hall.

Dale Warfel reported from the Central League meeting – 35 games to be played, each team 5 times. The league to begin on May 13th.

Ted Arnold reported on the borough council meeting. (**Author** – No information in the minutes on what was reported.)

The insurance company said that the bleachers must be repaired, high grass must be mowed, the score card must be repaired, junk must be cleared away from the bleachers, and the grass must be kept out of the infield.

It was decided to renew the insurance with Milt Baker for $185.00

The playground director will be Barry Shearer unless he gets another job. If so another director will be hired.

Work will be done on the diamond this week… practice will be on Saturday.

Membership drive to take place later in the summer.

Some player contracts were signed. Others will be signed at practice.

Trying to look into getting Lynn Henry for the Central League manager.

Ted Arnold was to look into getting the diamond and play-ground rolled.

It was decided to get the tractor fixed at Innerst's.

Next meeting scheduled for May 7th. (**Author**– No further meetings were recorded in the minutes for the year.)

January 28, 1962

Meeting was held in the Jacobus Fire Hall.

Elected officers for the year 1962:

President: Ted Arnold
Vice President: Lonnie Weaver
Recording Secretary: Barry Shearer
Financial Secretary: George Arnold
Treasurer: Norman Shearer Sr.
Director: Dale Warfel

Officers will go to the February meeting of the borough council to discuss what to do with the building used for storage of gang mowers and also the playground director's fee. It will also be recommended that they form a Recreation Association to take over all aspects of the playground.

An idea of starting a "100" club instead of having a carnival to make money was discussed. Possibly going in with the Fire Department on this and making it a "200" club.

Motion passed to place a team in the Central League for the 1962 season. Lee Arnold said that he thought he could get Chase Heaps to manage the team and was given the go-ahead.

Smith Village is expanding their sports department and have offered 10% discount on Spalding equipment and Adirondack bats. Pricing will also be done at Grove and Sechrist. Business will be split among more than one.

Motion carried that we pay cigarette license.

March 4, 1962

Meeting was held in the Jacobus Fire Hall.

Reporting that nothing definitely was decided at the borough council meeting.

Motion made that we get a playground director for 1962. Lonnie Weaver was being considered for the position.

It was decided to start selling tickets for the "200" club the 2nd or 3rd week in April.

New equipment would be purchased from both Smith's and Grove and Sechrist.

Heaps will be contacted about managing the Central League team. Keeping the insurance policy with Milt Baker.

April 8, 1962

Meeting was held in the Jacobus Fire Hall.

The "200" club will start April 23rd.

Chase Heaps will manage the teams this year. He said that he would bring as many players as we need.

Mark Innerst is going to check with Mr. Berger about pitching for us.

Nothing has been decided yet on a playground director.

Author - This was the last entry in the JAA minutes book.

Appendix C: Teams and Leagues

Some of the details about the different Leagues of the time, are in the sections below. Some of it can be a bit confusing, but the first section below is taken from the Athletic Association Minutes, so it's probably the best record of Jacobus's participation in each of the leagues.

- Beginning 1947 - Jacobus had a team in the **Greater York County League**. This team won the championship in 1947.

- January 1948 - It was decided to apply to the **Southern York County League**, the **Twilight League** and the **Greater York County League**. Preferences would be as listed."

(Author) - The Southern League and the Twilight league, were higher-level leagues than the Greater York County League.

- February 1948 - It was reported that the **Southern York County** and **Twilight Leagues** were both filled. The **Greater League** did not respond yet. After discussions, the Association decided to add a second team. Preparations, League and Manager will follow at a future meeting

- March 1948 - It was reported the first team will continue in the **Greater League**. It was also reported that the Jacobus second team will be in the newly formed **Western Baseball League**.

- January 1949 - George Keeney Jr. and Sid Straley attended a meeting of the **York Co. Twilight League** to see if there were any current openings, but it was reported that there were no berth's open at the moment but would be considered for a future opening.

- January 1949 - Motion was made and approved to try to get in the **Southern York County League** for 1949."
  (The first team was dissatisfied with the **Greater York Co. League**)

- January 1949 - The second team will stay in the **Western League**.

- February 1949 - Herbert Geiselman gave a report on the **Greater League** Meeting. Nevin Smith gave a report on the **Southern League** meeting, stating they have accepted our 1st team in the league. Therefore, holding a berth in two leagues. Herbert Geiselman said that he would notify the **Greater League** of our withdrawal.

- March 1949 - (**Author** – it appears from the minutes that recently the second team had moved to the **City County League**, but I did not see any specific reference to that previously in the minutes.) A report on the **City County League** was heard by Sid Straley, substituting for Carl D. Arnold. He said that the league has adopted the Goldsmith ball and no forfeit money was paid as of yet.

- February 1950 - A $15.00 check was granted to the treasurer of the **City County League** for the forfeit money of the second team, which had to be posted at the March 2nd meeting. (**Author** – second team was once again to be in the **City County League.** It appears that the "forfeit" money that is mentioned here and other places is the fee required to join a league.)

- March 1950 - The first team will continue in **the Southern York County League.**

- March 1951 - Grover Kirschner was selected to manage the first team in the **Southern York County League**. Indications are looking like the **City-County League** will be ready for the second team.

- April 1951 – (**Author** - It appears that the second team is now in the **City-County League**…) Red Arnold, President, will be **City-County League** Representative.

- January 1952 - Decided to sponsor three (3) baseball teams again in the same leagues.

- March 1952 - Paid $40.00 to the **Southern York County League** for our forfeit money.

- November 1952 - Received $24.60 from the **Southern York County League**. (Author – Although it does not say it, it appears that the Second Team was pulling out of the Southern York County League. Not sure where they went if anyplace.)

- March 1953 - It was announced that the application was accepted for a berth in the **Central York Co. League** (first team).

- January 27, 1954 - Motion was made to retain the berth in the **Central York Co. League** for the 1954 season.

- July 21, 1954 - A good deal of discussion as to having a second team next year to make a place for some of the younger players. Discussion was postponed until next spring. (**Author** – Up to this point I hadn't noticed that the second team was not in operation. Looking back, it appears that the last mention of a second team was back in November 1952. Not sure if this means anything or not.)

- February 21, 1955 - It was reported that the **Susquehanna league** would not accept our application because of the policy of the league not wanting teams from towns of more than one team. (**Author** – Is there still a second team in town at this point?)

Forfeit money for the **Central League** would be due on March 11.

- May 25, 1955 - A motion was made that we offer $2 to the men who will go along with the **second team**, to umpire for them. (**Author** – this is the first mention of the second team for a while. Evidently it still exists.)

- January 18, 1956 - It was decided that we enter teams in the **Central**, **Amateur**, and **Baseball for Boys**. (**Author** – Looks like the second team *does* still exist – now in the **Amateur** League.)

- January 29, 1958 - Motion made to enter teams in the four leagues we were in last year. (**Author** – Guessing these to be **Central League**, **Amateur League**, **Baseball for Boys 8 – 12**, and **Baseball for Boys 13 – 15**?)

- February 1, 1959 - Motion was made and seconded to have a team in the **Central League**.

- May 3, 1959 - It was decided to have a team in the **Amateur** League. Carl Folkenroth will serve as manager.

- May 1, 1960 - The manager of the **Central League** team this year will be William Heltzel. At this point the **Amateur League** team manager was not known.

- March 19, 1961 - It was announced that there would be two **Baseball for Boys** teams.

- January 28, 1962 - Motion passed to place a team in the **Central League** for the 1962 season.

- Per Gene Snyder, the **Central League** team folded in 1963.

Following are some random comments about the leagues from my Dad, Carl "Red" Arnold:

- "Early on we were originally in the Greater League. And then the minutes show that we were trying to get into the Southern League or the Twilight league, which were a little bit higher level teams. Like in the major and minor league baseball organizations. There was as low as a class D league. They were the lowest and then the C and B and then the AA and AAA. The Greater league was a county league. And then later on we got into the. Southern League"

- "Initially it was one team and then when we had younger people playing we formulated a second team and that was in the Western League and the City County League. In fact, I don't think I mentioned at all that I managed a couple of years there."

- "What was the name of the town... I can't think of it… where Perry Junior jumped into the pig pen to get a ball? Weiglestown? (**Author**) Uncle Ted later says that this was Wiota."

- "We had second teams from Lincoln Way and Reliance and West York and York New Salem and Lucky… There's a place over toward Stoverstown… I can't even think of it now, where the outfield was in the pig pen. (**Author**) Uncle Ted later says that this was Wiota. What was the name of that place beyond Stoverstown? ...Cly's up in York Haven... Lucky's down below Conrads. Outside of Stoverstown... it'll come to me... And then it was the City County League, and then after the City County League, I think there was a fourth...because of more teams being added there was just additional leagues."

Following are some random comments about the leagues from my uncles Lee and Bob Arnold:

- "The second team only allowed two players over twenty-one. We were in a City County league. This was all primarily high school kids or one or two years out of high school."

- "So, the difference between the first and second teams was primarily age."

- "The older guys are on the first team and the second team was younger guys? That's why you couldn't stack the second team with a bunch of experienced ballplayers. They were all expected to be, you know, younger, and not playing on the town's big team."

Following are some random comments about the leagues from my uncle Ted Arnold:

- "I graduated in '57. So, after I was done playing "Thirteen to fifteen" ... your Dad and I know this because he was a manager... they started what they called a York County Amateur League. And you were allowed two players over twenty-one. Everybody else had to be younger. And so, then after I was done playing thirteen fifteen… and I don't know when… they might have started that maybe when I was seventeen. So that would have been around fifty-seven …somewhere between fifty-seven and sixty I would imagine."

- "Then I think what they had was what they called the Central League, the Susquehanna League… maybe… See there was a Central League and then there was a York County League. There was a second team … that might have been the Amateur League. ... and I'm not sure when that disbanded…. And then that's when I went up to the "major leagues" (Uncle Ted laughs) … Up to the "big time" … That would have been the Central League (smiles)."

- "The Susquehanna League was like… Well it was like Loganville, Red Lion, Windsor… Spry was in the Central League…they had a very good team. They had guys that had a shot at playing professional ball. They were always Top Guns in the Central League."

- "The York County Amateurs…. We played…. Crispus Attucks had a team in the York County Amateurs. And that was an all black team… they might have had some white players, but yeah, that was an all black team."

- "We used to go… I think Lucky was in that league. No… that wouldn't have been York County Amateurs… Lucky was down towards the river… down below… down in the Conrad's area. Down below where Conrad's is. Yeah that's right, we used to play Conrad's. Conrad's always had a pretty good team in the York County amateurs."

- "Jacobus had a second team… That's when we played Wiota… we'd go to Wiota… we'd go to Admire. And they're north of. York… they're kind of up back of… You go up the old Susquehanna Trail and if you turn off to the left up there somewhere that would take you in to Admire. Wiota was over here towards. Jefferson."

- "Shrewsbury had a team. Glen Rock I think had a team. Just seems to me Jefferson that had a team... Oh. Seven Valleys had a team in the York County Amateur League. I do know that. Seven Valleys was in the York County Amateur League. So did Jacobus, Crispus Attucks, and I'm trying to think if Hallam had one. I know Hallam had a Thirteen to Fifteen team because we use to always have a good tussle with them... You know what… I think Hallam was in the York County Amateurs too."

- "I know Winterstown had a team. I remember going there. I guess that was the Central League… Manchester… Mount Wolf... they had baseball teams in the Central League. Pleasureville…. Manchester… there was also a team from New Holland (Author – in York County, not Lancaster County)"

- "And see then... and I don't know what they called that… you had the Central League. and then you had another League that Red Lion was in… Hallam was in… and Spry was in… I don't know how many teams were in that… and that was a better league…. that's back when my uncles were playing in that league. Uncle Sterling, Uncle Bill and Uncle Earl. Then you had that league and then you had the Central League… or maybe it was the York County League. I bet that's what it was. I think it was that league that Red Lion and Hallam and Windsor were in. I think it was in that better league. It was that league, and then they had the Southern York County League. And then I think what happened then… those two leagues kind of dispersed. And then… then you had the Central League. These two leagues kind of combined. Some of them dropped out and didn’t have teams anymore. And then you had what they called the Central League. And then maybe that's where the York County Amateur League came about then. And that came about because the younger guys... when they came out of thirteen to fifteen… they didn't have any place to play. And. And I think that’s how that team developed.”

- “The original baseball league… and that was the league that my uncles played in… Uncle Sterling played for Red Lion. Uncle Bill played for Spry. He pitched for Spry. And my Uncle Earl, he pitched for Seven Valleys. Red Lion, would load up their team from guys from all over the county. There was a guy from Red Lion… I don't know what his first name was… his last name was Horn. And he had money. In fact, their baseball diamond and football stadium were named after the family…. Red Lion stadium… I mean it had a big fence all the way around the outfield you know... And he would pay. Back then they had people that would pay for guys to come and play for them. And they were really good. Horn was good and he had the money… he was a big guy. He played first base.”

- "Jacobus didn't have too many paid players. I tell you most of the Jacobus team was local. Most of them were local. There was a guy named Les Williams (Lehman?). He came in and he managed for a couple years. And I kind of think he might have got paid because he was from another town. He was from Red Lion or Felton."

- "And then there was a guy from York… Stagemyer his name was. He was a pitcher and he pitched for us. And then we would get some kids from… well… some kids from college. That went to York College. In the summer they were looking for teams to play on and we had a couple… in fact two of them… Your Dad might remember these. Don Loucks was one of them… there was two of them that came out and inquired about you know whether they'd be able to play baseball with us. Don Loucks was one of them and I forget what the other guy's name was. So, they played a couple of years with Jacobus. And then there was one or two other guys too that I remember coming from York and playing out here."

- "I remember Wiota… One time I remember… I think it was Perry Innerst… someone hit a fly ball in center field and he had to go into the pig pen in center field… he had to go under the fence to get the ball…"

- "There was a family down there in Lucky… you know like here in Jacobus you had the Shearers and you had the Arnolds…Robertson's… there were a lot of Robertson's there in Lucky… and they were all good ball players"

(Author) – After checking with a local historian, Albert Rose, here's a clarification on the town names mentioned above… New Holland (York County), aka. Saginaw, was in the York Haven Area. Wiota was in N. Codorus Township in the area of Pigeon Hill – later known as Spring Grove

Appendix D: Trophy Case

Here are some photos, taken in July of 2017, of some of the baseball trophies located in the basement of the Jacobus Fire Hall. Thanks to Linette Snyder for allowing entrance to the Fire Hall, and for giving permission to see and photograph the trophies.

1947 Greater York County League Champs.

1947 Greater York County League Champs.

1949 City County League playoff winners

1949 City County League playoff winners

1950 City County League Champs

1951 Baseball for Boys Champs (13 – 15)

1952 Baseball for Boys Championship Runner-ups (13 – 15)

1953 Baseball for Boys Champs (13 – 15)

1953 Baseball for Boys Champs (13 – 15)

1953 Baseball for Boys Champs (13 – 15)

1954 Baseball for Boys Championship Runner-ups (13 – 15)

1958 Amateur League Champs

1958 Amateur League, Southern Div. Champs

1958 Amateur League, Southern Div. Champs

1958 Central League, Playoff Runner-ups

1958 Central League, Playoff Runner-ups

1967 League Champs, PASA Award

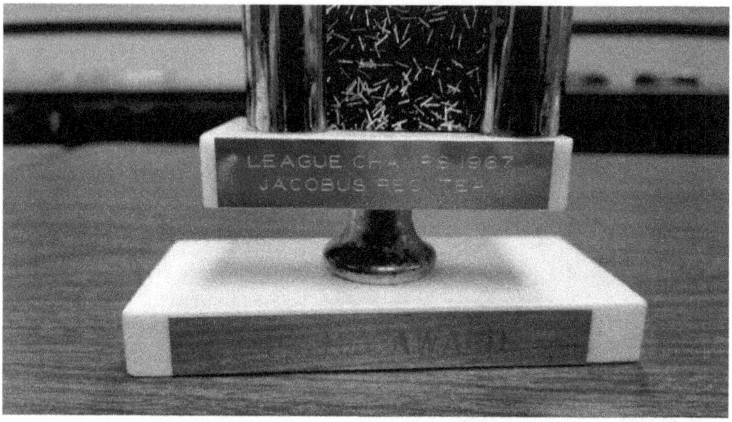

1967 League Champs, PASA Award

Trophy "treasure hunters", my Dad Carl Red Arnold and Uncle George Arnold, in the basement of the Jacobus Fire Hall.

Appendix E: The Roster (Early 1900's to early 1970's)

Here are the names of as many of the individuals involved with all of this, as the author could put together. This list of names was taken from those that appear in the Jacobus Athletic Association minutes and the other documents and news articles I was able to gather, and from the memories of those who were there back then. I'm sure that I don't have complete team lists.

Apologies to all of those who were left out of this list. I'm sure there were many others involved whose names I did not run into while doing the research. Other than spouses, only those family members are mentioned in the notes, who appear somewhere in the text of this book.

Also, to be fair, I decided not to include players from the mid-60s and early 70s teams. Although I remember quite a few names, there just was not enough time to compile a complete list. My emphasis for this project was on the 30s, 40s., 50s, and early 60s teams. I'll leave it up to others to complete this list.

Those with the designation – "*Original Jacobus Athletic Assoc. member" indicates that their names were mentioned in the very first Jacobus Athletic Association meeting minutes.

Last Name	First Name	Nick Name	Info
Allison	Mooney		1940s Teams
Allison	Whitey		1940s Teams
Arnold	William, A.	Bill	? Teams; Worked at American Chain & Cable Co. between E. Princess St. & Prospect St., York; Brother: Carl O. Arnold

Last Name	First Name	Nick Name	Info
Arnold	Carl, D.	Red	*Original Jacobus Athletic Assoc. member; Recreation Association member; 1940s Teams; Worked at Jacobus Plastics, Inc in Jacobus; Lived on farm near the current boat docks at Lake Redman, then later on Pine Street and Wildasin Drive; Wife: Ellenor Olp
Arnold	Earl		Pitched for Loganville; Brother: Carl O. Arnold
Arnold	George		Jacobus Athletic Assoc. member; 1950s, 1960s teams; Playground Director 1970's; Originally lived on farm near the current boat docks at Lake Redman; Father: Carl O. Arnold

Last Name	First Name	Nick Name	Info
Arnold	Marvin	Lee	Jacobus Athletic Assoc. member; Recreation Association member; 1940s, 1950s, 1960s teams; Basketball; Originally lived on farm near the current boat docks at Lake Redman; Father: Carl O. Arnold
Arnold	Paul		1950s, 1960s teams; Father William A. Arnold
Arnold	Richard	Rich	*Original Jacobus Athletic Assoc. member; 1940s Teams; Originally lived on farm near the current boat docks at Lake Redman. Was a milkman for Rutter's Dairy. Father: Carl O. Arnold

Last Name	First Name	Nick Name	Info
Arnold	Robert	Bob	1950's Teams; Originally lived on farm near the current boat docks at Lake Redman.
Arnold	Rodger		Jacobus Athletic Assoc. Member; ? Teams; Originally lived on farm near the current boat docks at Lake Redman; Father: Carl O. Arnold
Arnold	Sterling	Mule	Lived on the farm that is now known as Kain Park/Lake Redman. Was a salesman for York Machinery & Supply in York. Played in the minors with the St. Louis Cardinals organization; Brother: Carl O. Arnold

Last Name	First Name	Nick Name	Info
Arnold	Theodore	Ted	Jacobus Athletic Assoc. member; 1950s, 1960s teams; Originally lived on farm near the current boat docks at Lake Redman; Father: Carl O. Arnold
Arnold	William, A.		Pitched for Spry
Arnold	William, E.		*Possible* player on the 1908 team shown in 1987 Jacobus Centennial newspaper photo - Born in 1882. Could also possibly be a brother of William E.; Children: Carl O. Arnold
Arnold	Willie		? Teams; Father: William A. Arnold

Last Name	First Name	Nick Name	Info
Babble	Sam		Jacobus Athletic Assoc. member; He was a successful business man; Lived next to Stine's Barber Shop, (2) doors south of Clete Innerst on Main St. Served as fund raising Carnival Treasurer for several years; One of the biggest financial contributors to the Athletic Association organization.
Beck (Innerst)	Anita		Playground Director 1970's

Last Name	First Name	Nick Name	Info
Bohnert	Curtis		Jacobus Athletic Assoc. Member, 1955 carnival committee; Lives on Main St., Jacobus and worked for Spurg Miller, Automotive, his father-in-law; Brother: Ron
Bohnert	Ronald		Jacobus Athletic Assoc. member; 1950s Teams; Lived on Main Street two houses south of Leader's furniture; Wife: Darlene
Bohnert	Darlene		Jacobus Recreation Association - 1960's; Husband: Ron
Boyer	Harry		Elementary school teacher who lived on a farm south of Bob Wiley's Restaurant (a restaurant at the time along main street at the south end of town).
Brownie	P.		1930s Teams

Last Name	First Name	Nick Name	Info
Bupp	Charlie		Jacobus Athletic Assoc. member; Children: Richard
Bupp	C. Richard		Jacobus Athletic Assoc. member; 1940s, 1950s Teams; Basketball; He worked for Goodling Oil & Heating. Lived on Main Street (3) houses south of the Barber Shop; Father: Charlie Bupp
Chronister	Elwood		Lived outside of Jacobus. Was assigned to "get ball games".
Darr	Curtis		Jacobus Athletic Assoc. member; Lived on Water Street. He was a painter and artist.; Children: Jerry, Father: Benjamin Darr

Last Name	First Name	Nick Name	Info
Darr	Dallas		1930s Teams, He was People's Bank Manager and Postmaster of Jacobus. Lived on Pleasant Avenue west of the Post Office; Wife: Florence; Father: William Darr
Darr	Ed		1908 Team
Darr	Elaine		Jacobus Recreation Association member - 1960's; Husband: Roger
Darr	Jerry		Jacobus Athletic Assoc. member, ? Teams; Lived on Water Street.
Darr	William	Bill	Jacobus Recreation Association member; Lived on Water Street. Not a ball player.
Dellinger	Bertram	Bert	1908 Team; Lived on Main Street in Jacobus.
Dellinger	Richard	Dick	1940s Teams; Lived on Main Street in Jacobus; Father: Bert Dellinger

Last Name	**First Name**	**Nick Name**	**Info**
Diehl	Lee		? Teams
Diehl	Milt		1930s Teams; Was a butcher with his Dad in a Loganville Meat Market. Drove a meat truck door to door through the streets of Jacobus and Loganville.
Erwin	Paul		Playground Director 1970's
Falkenstine	Allen, P.	Hunce	*Original Jacobus Athletic Assoc member; Had a painting business. Lived on Main Street next to Dr. Krout. North on Main St. Dr. Krout lived (2) houses north of Water St.

Last Name	First Name	Nick Name	Info
Falkenstine	Robert	Bob	Jacobus Athletic Assoc.; 1940s Teams, Basketball; Lived on Main St. Played in American Legion League for Yankee Club team – Central PA Champs 1951; Father: Allen Falkenstine
Ferree	Caleb		*Original Athletic Assoc. member; Lived on Water Street. Did not play ball but attended association meetings.
Ferree	Ed		Jacobus Athletic Assoc. member; He was a mason contractor. He helped build the original ball field bleachers. He lived on Lake Road.
Folkenroth	Mary		Jacobus Recreation Association member - 1960's

Last Name	First Name	Nick Name	Info
Folkenroth	Carl	Hooks	*Original Jacobus Athletic Assoc. member; 1940s and 1950s Teams; Was a ball player and was very active with the Athletic Association organization. Lived across Main street from the Barber Shop. He pitched and played outfield. Wife: Mary Carolyn
Forry	Mugs		1930s Teams; Lived in the apartments north of Smith Village. North of Smith Village Furniture.

Last Name	First Name	Nick Name	Info
Franklin	Ben		Jacobus Athletic Assoc. member; Owner of Jacobus Plastics, Inc. Donated steel pipes for the original backstop on the current ball field. Lived on Valley Road, two houses above the Plastics Factory.
Franklin	Ben		Jacobus Athletic Assoc. member; Son of the owner of Jacobus Plastics, Inc. Lived on Valley Road, two houses above the Jacobus Plastics Factory.
Franklin	Robert	Bob	1940s Teams at Ollie Hess Farm field; Original owner of the house and property just beyond center field.; Father: Ben Franklin
Franklin	Denny		Community volunteer - 1960's
Geiselman	William	Bill	Jacobus Athletic Assoc. member.

Last Name	First Name	Nick Name	Info
Geiselman	Richard	Chick	1930s Teams
Geiselman	Elmer		*Original Jacobus Athletic Assoc. member; Had a plumbing business at the south end of Jacobus. Did not play ball but was very involved in the Athletic Association organization.; Father: Ferris Geiselman, Brother: John Geiselman
Geiselman	Herb		Lived four houses south of the barber shop. Was a milk man. Maybe played baseball in the 30's? and did concession work on the new baseball field in 1948.
Geiselman	John		Jacobus Recreation Association. Community historian.
Geiselman	Leon		Jacobus Athletic Assoc.

Last Name	First Name	Nick Name	Info
Geiselman	Vernon		1940s and 1950s Teams; Father: John Geiselman
Getz	Dr. John		Jacobus Athletic Assoc. member; Family doctor in Jacobus 40s and 50s; Lived on Main St. across from Nevin Smith.; He was the football team doctor and was always on the sidelines.
Heaps	Clase		Manager of the 1962 Central League team.
Heltzel	Bill	Heine	Lived on Lake Road. Had played some professional baseball with the Boston Braves. Played 3rd base for Jacobus after minor league career.
Heltzel	William	Jr.	Pitched for City County league; Central League; Father Bill Heltzel

Last Name	First Name	Nick Name	Info
Hershner	Preston	Pret	*Original Jacobus Athletic Assoc. member, 1940s and 1950s Teams; Managed the Jacobus 2nd team. Worked in a metal shop in York. Lived on Valley Road to the rear of Stan Kohr's property. Was a manager and a catcher.; Children: Steve Hershner
Hershner	Steve		Jacobus Athletic Assoc. member; 1940s and 1950s Teams batboy, Played on ? Teams locally; Played with Buffalo, a minor league team in the Philadelphia Phillies organization. Father: Preston Hershner

Last Name	First Name	Nick Name	Info
Hess	Ollie		Lived on the farm north end of Jacobus. His barn was where the Smith Village facility t is now. His property was the baseball field in the late 1940s, prior to the current field.
Hildebrand	William, H.	Bill	*Original Jacobus Athletic Assoc. member.; Scorekeeper for the 1930s teams.; Lived on Main St. across the street from Olp's Flower Shop. Was a ball team business manager and helped with maintenance work (grounds keeping).; Children: Earl (Easter) and Carroll

Last Name	First Name	Nick Name	Info
Hildebrand	Carroll		*Original Jacobus Athletic Assoc. member; 1940s Teams, Lived on Main St. across the street from Olp's Flower Shop. Mainly a business manager and umpire.; Father: Bill
Hildebrand	Clarke		1940s Teams
Hildebrand	Earl	Easter	*Original Jacobus Athletic Assoc. member.; 1930s, 1940s, and 1950s Teams.; Lived on Main St. across the street from Olp's Flower Shop. Played ball and managed. Father: Bill, Children: Larry
Hildebrand	Paul		Jacobus Athletic Assoc. member

Last Name	First Name	Nick Name	Info
Hullmann (Darr)	Patti		Playground Director 1970's

Last Name	First Name	Nick Name	Info
Innerst	Clete, L.		*Original Jacobus Athletic Assoc. member.; Lived on Main St. south of Smith Village Apartment and Auto Store. Business involved construction work, road work, and snow plowing. Association meetings were held at his business and his construction resources contributed greatly to the building and maintenance of the Jacobus Community Park.; Wife: Viola
Innerst	Dale		1950s and 1960s Teams; Basketball; Lived on Main Street across from the Fire Hall. Father: Ralph Innerst

Last Name	First Name	Nick Name	Info
Innerst	Mark		Jacobus Athletic Assoc. member; Playground Director - 1960's. Baseball for Boys All-Star 1957
Innerst	Pat		1930s Teams
Innerst	Perry, Jr.		1940s and 1950s Teams; His father owned Innerst Auto in Jacobus. He was also employed there.
Innerst	Ralph	Palley	*Original Jacobus Assoc. member; 19402 and 1950s Teams; Lived across Main Street from the fire hall. Corner of Main Street and Valley Road. Trucking and snow plowing. He was a manager and ball player.; Wife: Loretta Goodling, Children: Dale and Evelyn

Last Name	First Name	Nick Name	Info
Jamison	Sam		? Teams; Worked in the office at Leader's Furniture.
Keener	Melvin		Jacobus Athletic Assoc. member; Lived on Valley Road. Involved with organization but didn't play ball.
Keeney	George, Jr.	Juice	Jacobus Athletic Assoc. member; Lived at the south end of Jacobus. Helped with managing the business end of things, concessions, etc. He did not play ball.; Wife: Elizabeth Dellinger, Father: George Keeney, Sr.

Last Name	First Name	Nick Name	Info
Keeney	Jesse	Jet	1940s and 1950s Teams; Lived north of Manny Myer's blacksmith shop (north end of town.) Then later on Woodland drive. He played ball and was a catcher and out-fielder.; Wife: Charlotte, Father: George Keeney, Sr.
Keiser	Harry		*Original Jacobus Athletic Assoc. member; Lived on Valley Road. Became involved with the organization but didn't play baseball. Worked at American Chain and cable.; Children: Gerry Smeigh
Keiser	Ed		Community volunteer - 1960's

Last Name	First Name	Nick Name	Info
Keiser	Ken		*Original Jacobus Athletic Assoc. member; Active in the community and church. Never played ball. Lived on York Road. He was active to some extent in the association, he never played ball. None of his boys played baseball.; Wife: Helen
Kern	Donald	Duck	1950s Teams; Lived on Main Street two doors south of Dr. Getz's house.
King	Bud		1930s Teams
King	Jr.		Community volunteer - 1960's
Kirschner	Grover		Jacobus Athletic Assoc. member; 1950s Teams; Lived on Main Street south of Dr. Getz's house.

Last Name	First Name	Nick Name	Info
Kline	Bill		Jacobus Athletic Assoc. member; He was a sales-man and helped out with fund rais-ing Carnivals. Lived near N. J. Leaders. Did not play ball.
Kline	Glen		? Teams; Now lives on Woodland Drive.
Klinedinst	Robert		Jacobus Athletic Assoc. member.
Kohr	Stan		Jacobus Athletic Assoc. member; He had a radio/TV repair business. He lived on Pine Street. He didn't play ball but was a member of the or-ganization. Father: Curvin Kohr (had a grocery store on the corner of Main Street and Water Street.)

Last Name	First Name	Nick Name	Info
Krout	Dr. George		The only medical doctor in Jacobus at the time (30's, 40's.) Lived on Main Street (2) doors north of Water St. Did not play ball.
Lacondro	John		Mentioned as being on the town football team.
Leader	Nester		1930s Teams; On baseball picture and operator of the Leader Furniture Store. Children: N.J. Leader II
Lehman	Clinton	Clinty	Jacobus Athletic Assoc. member; Barber on Main Street in Jacobus, (5) houses south of Church Rd. Did not play ball but was a business man and umpire and supported the organization. Wife: Ruth
Lehman	Les		1940s Teams ?; Possibly lived in West York?

Last Name	First Name	Nick Name	Info
Lentz	Russell		1908 Team
Loucks	Don		? Teams
Loucks	Lester		? Teams
Markey	Charles		? Teams
McDonald	Dub		1930s Team; From Maryland. Brother: Lieb McDonald
McDonald	Lieb		1930s Team; From Maryland. Brother: Dub McDonald
McLaughlin	Clarence		? Teams
McLaughlin	Harry		The McLaughlin's lived on a farm north of Jacobus along the Codorus Creek. Made $10 donation noted in AA minutes.
McWilliams	Dennis		? Teams; Father: Palmer
McWilliams	Palmer		? Teams
McWilliams	Robert		? Teams; Father: Palmer
Meyers	Harvey		1908 Team

Last Name	First Name	Nick Name	Info
Meyers	Jake		Jacobus Athletic Assoc. member; He worked as a building contractor. Father: Sterling Meyers
Myers	Merlin	Speck	1930s Teams; Was a masonry contractor and served on the Dallastown School Board for several years.
Myers	Sterling, C.	Goose	*Original Jacobus Athletic Assoc. member; He worked as a building contractor.; Children: Rupp (real name?) and Jake
Miller	S., S.		Jacobus Athletic Assoc. member; Not sure if this is Spurg or not. Mentioned as Business Manager 1950.
Myers	Bill		1908 Team
Myers	Ervin		Jacobus Athletic Assoc. member; 1955 carnival committee

Last Name	First Name	Nick Name	Info
Myers	LeRoy	Fatty	Jacobus Athletic Assoc. member; 1930s and 1940s Teams; Lived on York Road across from the first baseball diamond. Worked for C. M. Parr company, right off of Rt. 30 and N. George St. and was a borough tax collector. Played ball as a catcher. Umpire in the 1940s.; Wife: Charlotte Dietz
Ness	Walter		? Teams; Lived in Loganville.
Olp	Howard		*Original Jacobus Athletic Assoc. member; Worked at Heilig's Wire and Cloth. Also established Mickley & Olp's Flower Shop. He worked at the ballgame concession stand. Wife: Myrtus Mickley

Last Name	First Name	Nick Name	Info
Olp	Robert		Jacobus Athletic Assoc. member; local business-man; 1955 carnival commit-tee
Poff	Jean		Jacobus Recrea-tion Association. 1960's.
Reish	John		Playground Direc-tor – 1960's
Rohrbaugh	Don	Pepper	*Original Jacobus Athletic Assoc. member; 1940s Teams; Lived on York Road where the old ball dia-mond used to be. Baseball pitcher.; Wife: Jackie Stump
Rohrbaugh	Sal		1908 Team
Schmucker	R.		Playground Direc-tor - 1960's
Schroll	John		Concession stand - opening day

Last Name	First Name	Nick Name	Info
Schrum	Gerald	Schrummy	1940s and 1950s Teams; Lived in Bupp's Union area.
Shearer	Addison		1908 Team
Shearer	Arthur	Pete	*Original Jacobus Athletic Assoc. member; ? Teams; Played baseball and was a catcher. He was a plumber.; Wife: Beatrice, Father: Solomon Shearer
Shearer	Barry		Jacobus Athletic Assoc. member; 1950s and 1960s Teams; Father: Fritz Shearer
Shearer	Clarke	Jake	*Original Jacobus Athletic Assoc. member; 1940s and 1950s Teams; Active with the second team (Western League). Later on, lived on Woodland Drive. Father: Solomon Shearer

Last Name	First Name	Nick Name	Info
Shearer	Dane		1950s, 1960s teams; Father Fred Shearer
Shearer	Dennis		? Teams; Father Norman Shearer
Shearer	Erwin	Buzzard	Jacobus Athletic Assoc. member; 1930s Teams
Shearer	Fred, S.	Fritz?	Possible 1930s player. Fred S. Shearer is the father of Russ Shearer. Children: Russ and William (Bill), Father: Solomon Shearer
Shearer	Fred, C.		Jacobus Athletic Assoc. member; Possible 1930s player.; Father: Solomon Shearer
Shearer	Jack		1950s Teams ?; Lived on a farm where Lake Redman is now located. Played ball. Father: Fred Shearer

Last Name	First Name	Nick Name	Info
Shearer	Norman	Bud	Jacobus Athletic Assoc. member; 1950s Teams; Father: Solomon Shearer
Shearer	Larry		Playground Director - 1950's and 1960's
Shearer	Ray, Jr.	Junie?	Lived in Jacobus. Basketball, Played Legion ball then some in the minor leagues in the Boston Braves organization. Father: Ray Shearer, Sr.
Shearer	Russ, Sr.		Jacobus Athletic Assoc. member; 1940s and 1950s Teams; Lived on a farm where Lake Redman is now located. He was a baseball player. Father: Fred Shearer
Shearer	Solomon	Sol	1908 Team; Lived on the corner of Main and Meadow Street across from Smith Village.; Wife: Tillie

Last Name	First Name	Nick Name	Info
Shearer	William	Bill	1940s and 1950s Teams; Lived on a farm where Lake Redman is now located. Played ball.
Sherrick	Diane		Playground Director - 1960's
Shirey	Mick		? Teams
Shive	Cletus		Jacobus Athletic Assoc. member; He was a farmer and general laborer. He lived on Water Street. Grounds keeper at the ball diamond.
Shive	Glenn		Jacobus Athletic Assoc. member
Sipe	Ron		? Teams
Slenker	Don		Jacobus Athletic Assoc. member; Brother of Mervin Slenker
Slenker	Mervin, Jr.		Jacobus Athletic Assoc. member

Last Name	First Name	Nick Name	Info
Smeigh	Jon		Jacobus Athletic Assoc. member; 1955 carnival committee
Smith	Bruce		Owner of Smith Village Co.
Smith	Charlie		1940s and 1950s Teams; Moved to Jacobus from Maryland. Lived on Valley road (2) doors west Jacobus Plastics Factory.
Smith	Clair		*Original Jacobus Athletic Assoc. member; He was a truck driver, hauled coal, and was a building contractor. Wife: Madelin
Smith	Danny		Basketball; Father: Raymond Smith
Smith	Dallas		Community volunteer - 1960's

Last Name	First Name	Nick Name	Info
Smith	Donald		Jacobus business-man - Smith Village Co.; Con-tributed financially and very active with the Jacobus Rec-reation Association
Smith	John		Playground Direc-tor 1970's
Smith	Karl	Bud	*Original Jacobus Athletic Assoc. member; 1940s Teams; Did farm-ing the major part of his life on his Dad's property. Oldest son of Mont Smith. Would haul truck-loads of strawberries to Hershey to make ice cream. Father: Mont Smith

Last Name	First Name	Nick Name	Info
Smith	Larry		Jacobus Athletic Assoc. member; 1950s Teams, Basketball; Lived on Water Street; Father: Raymond Smith
Smith	Mont		Jacobus Athletic Assoc. member; His farm covered a good bit of Jacobus, south of Smith Village and off Pleasant Avenue. The property included the current baseball field and Salem UCC Church locations.

Last Name	First Name	Nick Name	Info
Smith	Nevin		*Original Jacobus Athletic Assoc. member; Basket-ball; He owned a meat market in York on S. Pershing Ave. He lived across from Dr. Getz on Main Street. One of the biggest financial contributors to the organization. Wife: Pauline, Father: Mont Smith
Smith	Paul	Jake	*Original Jacobus Athletic Assoc. members; 1940s Team; Did construction work. Built houses in Jacobus, Leader's Heights, Spry, and Shrewsbury. He was also a truck driver and hauled coal. Wife: Margie, Father: Mont Smith

Last Name	First Name	Nick Name	Info
Smith	Raymond		Jacobus Athletic Assoc. member; 1954 carnival committee; worked for Plitt's soda mfg.; Wife: Dorothy Smith
Snyder	Gene		Jacobus Athletic Assoc. member; 1940s, 1950s, and 1960s Teams; Basketball; Managed Jacobus for two years 1960 - 61. Lived on Main Street close to the Methodist Church. The House is no longer there. Brother of Gerry, Jay, and Ronnie Snyder
Snyder	Gerry		1940s and 1950s Teams; Basketball; Lived on Main Street close to the Methodist Church. The House is no longer there. Brother of Gene, Jay, and Ronnie Snyder

Last Name	First Name	Nick Name	Info
Snyder	Jay		Jacobus Athletic Assoc. member; 1940s and 1950s Teams, Basketball; Lived on Main Street close to the Methodist Church. The House is no longer there. Bat Boy for 40's team. Brother of Gene, Gerry, and Ronnie Snyder
Snyder	Ronald	Ronnie	1950s Teams; Lived on Main Street close to the Methodist Church. The House is no longer there. Brother of Gene, Gerry, and Jay Snyder

Last Name	First Name	Nick Name	Info
Straley	Sid		*Original Jacobus Athletic Assoc. member; Basketball; Lived on Main Street and later Valley Road. He worked for Pensupreme Milk and delivered house to house. Didn't play ball but was very active in the various organizations. Wife: Grace
Statler	Owen		Playground Director - 1960's
Stremmel	Robert		Baseball for Boys All-Star 1957
Trout	Barbara		Playground Director - 1960's
Trout	Clair		1930s Teams; School teacher and high school principal at Dallastown High School.
Van Artsdalen	Lyrian		Playground Director 1970's

Last Name	First Name	Nick Name	Info
Wagner	Richard	Dickey	1950s Teams; From Glen Rock. Wife: Deanna Myers
Warfel	Dale		? Teams
Warfel	John, A.		1940s and 1950s Teams; Lived at what is now Nixon Park.; Father: John Warfel
Warfel	Roy	Dink	1940s Teams; Lived at what is now Nixon Park. Played ball. Got paid as a pitcher.; Father: John Warfel
Weaver	Lonnie		? Teams; Considered for possible playground director
Weaver	Ronnie		? Teams
Whitman	Rick		Playground Director 1970's
Williams	Less		1950s Teams
Wildasin	Sam		Community volunteer - 1960's
Wise	Dale		1950s Teams; Lived in Dallastown. Pitched for Jacobus for a few games in 1955

Last Name	**First Name**	**Nick Name**	**Info**
Wolf	Edward		1908 Team; Lived in Leader's Heights.
Zartman	Chris		Playground Director 1970's

Appendix F: Local Baseball Dynasties and the Arnold Family

The Arnold family in Jacobus had a small baseball dynasty in the 40s and 50s and early 60s. The article shown later, which appeared in the Lancaster Sunday News on July 29th, 1962, describes that at one time four of my uncles and my Dad were playing on a Jacobus team. In addition, before that, my Dad's uncles Sterling, Earl, and Bill also played ball in the area. As mentioned in the chapter entitled "Beginnings", Sterling was involved in professional baseball for a period of time.

As an example, from earlier in this book, here are the second and first teams from 1958, with all of the Arnolds highlighted.

Amateur League Champs (second team) – **George Arnold, Paul Arnold**, **Roger Arnold**, **Ted Arnold**, **William Arnold**, Barry Shearer, Gene Shearer, Dane Shearer, Merv Slenker (Mgr.), Whitey Kershner (coach), Jerry Darr, Pete Klein, Frank Curry, M.Dise, Don Smith, Barry Shearer, Jack Shearer, Dale Warfle, **Don Arnold** (Scorer), Don Slenker (Scorer).

Central League Runner-ups (first team) – D. Innerst (Dale), N. Shearer (Norman (Bud)), R. Shearer (Russell), L. Williams (Les), G. Snyder (Gerry)?, C. Folkenroth (Carl), R. Riese (Ronald), M. Keeney (Jess (Min)), D. Kerns (Donald (Duck)), J. Snyder (Jay), **R. Arnold (Richard)**, R. Bohnert (Ronald), A. Shearer (Arthur (Pete)), B. Shearer (Barry), Gene Snyder, **L. Arnold (Lee)**, D. Stagemyer (Donald)

If you took notice, there are a lot of Shearers on the above team rosters also. The Shearer family was another dynasty in Jacobus athletics during the time covered by this book.

Beginning in the mid-60s the number of Arnolds participating in Jacobus sports dwindled. Some in the next generation of Arnold's had the potential athletic ability to play baseball, but eventually the dynasty ended. We all had other directions and talents to pursue instead. Many of my uncles and their families gradually left town and moved to other locations. If there were any baseball dynasties left in Jacobus after the mid-1960s, it would probably have been the Shearer or Snyder families.

Baseball — A Tradition With Arnold Family

By TOM KEESEY

When it comes to playing baseball, the Arnold family of Jacobus will take a back seat to no one. Over the past 10 years no less than eight sons of Mr. and Mrs. Carl Arnold have been playing baseball for Jacobus. At one time five of the brothers were playing on the same team, and right now three are playing in the Central League.

The oldest brother Carl (or Red) started the long chain of Arnolds when he began catching for Jacobus. Then came Rich, Bob, Lee, Rog, Ted, George and Don. Only Lee, George and Ted are still playing for Jacobus.

Rich and Lee played their early baseball for the Yankee team in the American Legion League and played in several play-off games. Ted and George were members of the Glen Rock Legion team. At one time Red, Bob, Ted, George and Don played on the same Jacobus team. Bob, however, injured his back while in the army and confines his activity to keeping score except in cases of emergency when his services are needed.

POP NOT PLAYER

Strangely enough, Papa Arnold was not an active player in the county. His sons interest in baseball was assisted by their three uncles, Sterling, Earl and Bill. All three were pitchers and Sterling pitched in the minor leagues.

"They started taking us to games when the interest in county baseball was high and we just naturally wanted to play the game," Lee commented. "Dad always came to our games and always stressed teamwork by asking us how many errors or strikeouts we had instead of how many hits."

Of the three Arnolds now active, Lee is probably the most consistent hitter, batting around .290. This season he switched from the outfield to catching and prefers the duties behind the plate. George, a catcher before this season now plays the outfield along with brother Ted. Ted is also a pitcher and had a 7-1 mark in the Amateur League in 1958 when Jacobus won the title. Lee's best season was in 1951 when he batted .397. Acousin, Bill Arnold, is also a member of the team this year.

The Arnold's baseball activity is not only confined to the playing field. As is the case with most of the local teams in this era they also have to see that the players are signed to contracts, take care of the ball diamond before and after each game and arrange for the finances to run the ball team each year. Without their services and those like them through the county, amateur baseball would not be a part of the summer sports calendar.

Baseball is almost a year around activity with the three Arnolds. eorge is president of the Jacobus baseball association, Ted is the financial secretary and Lee, was a former president and is now a member of the board of directors. As officers of the association they cooperate with other members of the community to raise funds for Jacobus's three teams, the 8-12, 13-15 and the Central League team.

Whenever the Arnolds have a family get together baseball is the favorite topic with the three Yankee fans being outnumbered by the Yankee haters. The number of playing Arnolds is down to three but a new generation of five in number, now is on the way and the Jacobus ball team will probably have a few Arnolds in the lineup for a long time.

Article appearing in the Lancaster Sunday Newspaper article on July 29, 1962

Ted Arnold, left and George Arnold, right give their full attention as brother Lee shows
how he grips ball to throw runners out steal ing.

Uncles Ted, Lee, and George appearing in the Lancaster Sunday Newspaper article on July 29, 1962

Uncle Lee, my Dad Red, and Uncle Bob around 1950. (Photo courtesy of Carl Arnold)

Uncle Rich around 1950. (Photo courtesy of Carl Arnold)

The author, ready for action. July 1956. (Photo courtesy of Carl Arnold)

www.ingramcontent.com/pod-product-compliance
Lightning Source LLC
Chambersburg PA
CBHW031235090426
42742CB00007B/202
* 9 7 8 1 7 3 2 2 5 3 2 1 6 *